Group
Portrait

Also by Nicholas Delbanco

Group Portrait

Joseph Conrad, Stephen Crane,
Ford Madox Ford, Henry James,
and H. G. Wells

Nicholas Delbanco

WILLIAM MORROW AND COMPANY

New York   *1982*

"Figures in a Landscape" appeared in *Antaeus* magazine.

The author gratefully acknowledges the John Simon Guggenheim Memorial Foundation for support during the writing of this book.

Library of Congress Cataloging in Publication Data

Delbanco, Nicholas.
  Group portrait.

  Includes bibliographical references and index.
  1. Novelists, English—20th century—Biography.
  2. Novelists, American—20th century—Biography.
  3. Kent—Biography.   4. East Sussex—Biography.
  I. Title.
PR105.D4   823′.912′09 [B]   81–16787
ISBN 0–688–01017–2   AACR2

Printed in the United States of America

First Edition

1 2 3 4 5 6 7 8 9 10

BOOK DESIGN BY MICHAEL MAUCERI

For Richard Elman

who has represented, from the first,
the collegiality this book proposes

Acknowledgments

In a book about colleagueship, the community one wants to thank is large; my debts are general as well as specific. From the casual remark to close reading of the typescript, I have had continual help. Strangers have willingly offered their aid, and scholars their attention. My friends, associates, and family have been supportive throughout. It is not, therefore, simple to single out those I wish especially to thank. But let me name a few.

James Landis of William Morrow and Company has shaped this manuscript and has shared in the project as only a trusted editor can; Sonia Greenbaum copyedited *Group Portrait* with meticulous exactitude. John Hawkins and Gail Hochman of Paul R. Reynolds, Inc., have been agents in the tradition established by the Paul Reynolds who supported Stephen Crane; it is a pleasure to report that the tradition continues. My students at the University of Iowa in 1979 and at Bennington College one year later kept me to the mark; their enthusiasm for such a course of study helped sustain my own.

Those who responded to portions of the text, or read it in its entirety, include: James Atlas, Alan Cheuse, Richard Elman, Stanley Eskin, Kathryn Frank, Claude Fredericks, Robert Foulke, John Gardner, Suzanne Levine, Jonathan Levy, Frank MacShane, Geoffrey Norman, Marjorie Pryse, Dave Smith, Mark Vaughan, and Jon Manchip White. Each and all of these have mattered more than they know, or than such a listing can suggest. I am grateful to Janice Biala and to the Trustees of the Joseph Conrad Estate for permission to quote from the work of Ford Madox Ford and Joseph Conrad, respectively. Material in Chapter IV from *Henry James and H. G. Wells,* edited by Leon Edel and Gordon H. Ray, is reprinted by permission of William Morris Agency, Inc., on behalf of Leon Edel. Of special assistance also, and deserving a special acknowledgment, are the staffs of the following libraries: Bennington College, Columbia University, The University of Illinois at Champaign-Urbana, Princeton University, The University of Texas at Austin, and the University of Virginia at Charlottesville.

Richard and Alice Stevenson offered their house in Kent with the kind of generosity that beggars thanks; my brother Andrew and my wife, Elena, are two close critics indeed. Gertrude Stein's pronouncement "I write for myself and for strangers" states only two thirds of the case. One writes for a trusted audience also—those ears that correct intonation and eyes that hold the line.

Contents

Group
Portrait

I.

Figures in
a Landscape

---

*As a general rule we do not want much
encouragement to talk about ourselves; yet
this little book is the result of a friendly
suggestion, and even of a little friendly
pressure. I defended myself with some
spirit; but, with characteristic tenacity, the
friendly voice insisted, "You know, you
really must."*

—JOSEPH CONRAD, "A Familiar Preface"
to *A Personal Record,* 1923

I.
Figures in
a Landscape

Novelists avoid collaboration. Yet they also exalt it. Many workers work alone, but not all need aspire always to be soloists. A masterpiece of English prose—the King James Version of the Bible—was written by committee. The performing arts require a community and immediate audience; painters and musicians have often somehow seemed to have a sense of joint endeavor, so that we think of them as in each other's studios after lunch. Dancers, too, appear to move in schools and shoals. But the image of a writer remains that of a solitary—splendid or churlish, coming out of isolation to get drunk or go on talk shows, and always, irreducibly, alone. For fiction-writing is a privacy made public. Hardy, Melville, and Tolstoy knew their fellow novelists, but each would have scoffed at the notion of a group—or any school not of their own teaching.

It is all the more remarkable, therefore, when writers do

cluster together. And in our century there have been at least two such noted occasions: Paris in the twenties, and the Bloomsbury group. Yet critical attention can overweight the scale. Much has been written about Hemingway and Fitzgerald at Gertrude Stein's, and the gossip value of Lytton Strachey's attentions to Vanessa Stephen is no longer high. The names of the bartender at the Crillon and Carrington's third cousin are, after all, less than crucial. In some curious fashion, the whole has come to seem more than the sum of the parts. The phenomenon of Bloomsbury or expatriate America begins to be as interesting as the work produced.

Whether these associations have been oversold of late is not, however, my concern; what's clear is that magic attaches to the notion of an artistic community. And the magic is strong. There are other instances, of course, and locales: Vienna, San Francisco, Buenos Aires . . . Alliances are being forged and broken as of this writing, but we have small perspective as yet; no matter what the manifestos or the manifest friendships and enmity, it is simpler to define a group in retrospect. This book attempts to do so. For it is my contention that those "noted occasions" are and should be no more notable than that of a third such grouping. South of London, in 1900, a galaxy of talent assembled that beggars in accomplishment anything the English language has since produced. Remarkably, too, they were writers first and last. The group has none of the interdisciplinary incoherence that comes when musicians paint pictures or economists describe ballet. To name the principals is to name enduring authors; to remind ourselves that they were in near daily contact is to raise the question these pages will address.

Joseph Conrad, Stephen Crane, Ford Madox Ford, Henry James, and H. G. Wells were, in 1900, neighbors.

Ford was then still using his given surname, Hueffer, but he shall be referred to here by his later chosen name. They lived in Kent and East Sussex; a day's brief journeying can circumscribe them all. Conrad at Postling, Crane at Brede, Ford at Aldington, James at Rye, and Wells at Sandgate form this portrait's group. Their nearness was no accident. Conrad rented Ford's house, Crane came at a mutual friend's suggestion. Rudyard Kipling was resident in Burwash down the road; such authors as John Galsworthy and W. H. Hudson passed through. It is not a question of mere geography, the way ten excellent artists might be living at any given moment in a ten-block sector of New York. This was a conscious retreat, a place of exile that amounted—for none of these men was native to the region—to elected home. In those days before the telephone, proximity to London helped; they took the train to the city for lunch. But theirs was no summertime country enclave; it was where they settled to work. In such a polyglot and multinational community (Hudson had been raised in Argentina, Kipling in India, Conrad in Poland, James and Crane in America), there was that sense of shared endeavor we credit to Bloomsbury or Paris, and of which a "movement" is made.

Conrad and Ford were collaborators. Ford reminisced much later on their protracted labor:

> We would write for whole days, for half nights, for half the day or all the night. We would jot down passages on scraps of paper or on the margins of books, handing them one to the other or exchanging them. We would roar with laughter over passages that would have struck no other soul as humorous; Conrad would howl with rage and I would almost sigh over others that no other soul perhaps would have found as bad as we considered them. We would recoil one from the other and go each to

our own cottage—our cottages at that period never being
further the one from the other than an old mare could
take us in an afternoon. In those cottages we would pre-
pare other drafts and so drive backwards and forwards
with packages of manuscript under the dog-cart seats.
We drove in the heat of summer, through the deluges of
autumn, with the winter snows blinding our eyes. But
always, always with manuscripts. Heavens, don't my
fingers still tingle with the feeling of undoing the stiff
buckles, long past midnight, of a horse streaming with
rain—and the rubbing down in the stable and the backing
the cart into the coach-house. And with always at the
back of the mind, the consideration of some unfinished
passage, the puzzledom to avoid some too-used phrase
that yet seemed hypnotically inevitable.[1]

James wrote of Conrad at length and was treated with
"almost oriental politeness" in return. Crane's last letter
was an attempt to secure a place on the Queen's list for
the impoverished Conrad. Such generosity was standard.
Wells records that James (with Edmund Gosse in tow)
paid him an early visit in order to assess the younger
man's financial needs; Ford openhandedly promoted his
peers. No author of our era, with the possible exception of
Ford's friend and protégé, Pound, was such an entrepreneur. Crane shattered a plate with his revolver when
someone suggested that Conrad's "The Nigger of the
'Narcissus' " had failed; later, when someone observed that
he'd had the ill commercial luck to be born in Kipling's
time, Crane agreed: "Yes. I'm just a dry twig on the edge
of the bonfire."[2] Galsworthy called Hudson, "Of living
writers that I read, the rarest spirit . . . the most valuable
our Age possesses."[3] The author of *The Forsyte Saga*
would lend his London house for the birth of Conrad's
son.

Ford wrote at book-length on Conrad and James;

Conrad wrote essays on Crane and James; Wells wrote about them all. Inveterate biographers and autobiographers, they have left much language behind. There were letters, volumes, and dedications exchanged, plans formed and shelved, agents shared. These men took trips together, formulated joint aesthetics, wrote books in the same room. If only to point out the degree to which their careers were linked and to remind the reader of such linkage, this book may serve a purpose. One thesis of *Group Portrait* is that something in the place and period caused talent to flourish as rarely before. At the very least it was coincidence; more likely it was more.

England, though an empire, was insular and hierarchical. These men were scarcely members of the cultured ruling class. Their very withdrawal from London—and not to such havens as Oxford or Cambridge—demonstrates as much. No member of the group was outlaw to the degree of Oscar Wilde, perhaps, but each of them was at odds with expectation. The distance Wells traveled from his childhood in cramped servants' quarters to the ownership of Spade House had already been immense. The aristocratic Conrad was living in near penury after a career at sea, unable to return to Poland and unwilling to return to France. James and Crane were made much of in England in part because they left America behind. Ford's lifelong fascination with the model of the English gentleman bespeaks an outsider's longing; as the "Pre-Raphaelite youth," Hueffer, he styled himself a renegade. The English novel was self-consciously reinvented by a band of foreigners who chose to emulate the French.

They knew themselves in opposition. The world of literary London, its clubs and power brokers, looked at them askance or with the kind of tolerance that incorporates disdain. And at the start of their careers (before they in turn became "established") they could take advantage of the license. An artist may violate decorum as does the fool in court. Crane understood this freedom and described it in *The O'Ruddy*. Outlandishly costumed and attended by his Sancho Panza, Paddy, our hero fights a duel:

> I came to understand the English character somewhat. The great reason was that Paddy and I were foreigners. It is not to be thought that gentlemen of their position would have walked out for a duel with an Englishman in the party of so fantastic an appearance. They would have placed him at once as a person impossible and altogether out of their class. They would have told a lackey to kick this preposterous creation into the horse pond. But since Paddy was a foreigner he was possessed of some curious license and his grotesque ways could be explained fully in a simple phrase: " 'Tis a foreigner."[4]

A proper man, Ford averred, could eat his lunch outside year-round if given a protecting wall to keep out wind and rain. The Gulf Stream runs sufficiently near to allow this region escape from the forbidding chill that grips the north of England. Fig trees grow, and mimosa, and the occasional palm. It is a fertile landscape and well-farmed; apple orchards and fields of hops abound. Vegetables grow in Romney Marsh; the hillsides are close-cropped by sheep. The pastures are ample for cows. Potatoes can be harvested in August. Oasthouses rise from every farm, and larger farms have several, their conical brick shapes topped by a white wooden cap. White weatherboard is characteristic of Kent; the villages are gaily variegated. A Georgian brick house will abut an Elizabethan half-timbered pub; behind them rises the stone vaulting of a medieval church. It is a democratic muddle, a gallimaufry, a place where foreigners have felt at home since Hastings.

That battle itself took place at Battle. A ruined Norman castle stands above the cliff at Hastings, and martello towers dot the shore. A Roman lighthouse at Dover may well be the oldest standing building in England, and Roman roads traverse the public footpaths still. But the sea has withdrawn. Rye and Winchelsea, those once proud ports, survey the Channel from a distance; their harbors hold pleasure boats only. Villages as far inland as Tenterden, or Smallhythe where Ellen Terry lived, were once harbors; a good ten miles of winding lanes now separate Smallhythe from the coast. Old Romney was a flourishing town on the River Rother; in the thirteenth century, however, its access silted up. Lydd was once an island, but its seaport grew so thick with shingle that it and the mainland have joined.

The castles keep. Bodiam was reconstructed by Lord Curzon so as to retain its ruined aspect; Scotney Castle was pulled down with selective care so that the remaining walls are "picturesque." That England is a garden has been a commonplace since Shakespeare and was not news to him; the gardens of Kent and East Sussex are everywhere impressive. (A later pair of writer-residents, Harold Nicolson and Vita Sackville-West, created a famous garden at Sissinghurst. That other local Bloomsbury shrine, Charleston—the home of Clive and Vanessa Bell and Duncan Grant—is well-planted also.) Ford's "small producer" who feeds himself year-round from his own kitchen garden is a quintessentially English figure, though seasoned in Provence.

The border of Kent and East Sussex is a landscape they all loved. The hill that halted Kipling's motorcar, the seawall and marshes, the valley that Galsworthy trotted ten miles through (talking all the while to companions in the dogcart), the lanes where Henry James, tangled in his dog's long leash, would, talking, walk—these things remain. Crane played marbles on the stone floor of his fourteenth-century manor; Ford tended his garden with pride. The just sufficiently wild sanctuary, the smell of salt air where the ocean withdrew—the knowledge more than nine hundred years later that Guillaume le Conquérant pitched camp near the Cinque Ports and taught the natives a new tongue—all this invigorates the visitor today. It is easy to feel and hard to ignore what James must have felt when he first approached Lamb House: here is a place one might work. When settled, James wrote his sister-in-law:

> All the good that I hoped of the place has, in fine, profusely bloomed and flourished here. It was really about the end of September, when the various summer supernumeraries had quite faded away, that the special note of Rye, the feeling of the little hilltop community bound together like a very modest, obscure and impecunious, but virtuous and amiable family began most unmistakably to come out . . . But the great charm is the simply *being* here, and in particular the beginning of the day no longer with the London blackness and foulness, the curtain of fog and smoke that one has each morning muscularly to lift and fasten back; but with the pleasant, sunny garden outlook, the grass all haunted with starlings and chaffinches, and the in-and-out relation with it that in a manner gilds and refreshes the day. This indeed—with work, and a few, a very few people—is the *all*.[5]

Impressionism is a term more current in art history than in prose. In the latter context—or as these men employed it—it describes selective presentation. Through a compound of memory with witnessed event, they sought to render what Conrad had called "the highest kind of justice to the visible universe." His celebrated phrase insists that the task is "before all, to make you see."[6] It is a process of association, or advance by indirection, and it served them well. It is *Group Portrait's* technique.

There is much to glean still, and much to fill in, for the portrait is selective. Many figures on the fringes of the group—R. B. Cunninghame Graham, the Garnett family, George Gissing, for instance—would repay close attention. The literary agent James B. Pinker is part of the community, if at a remove. And writers such as Arnold Bennett and Edith Wharton, who led their creative lives elsewhere, are importantly Edwardian and belong to this cadre. But I cannot hope to describe the community fully; the guest book of Lamb House alone would take several chapters to fill.

James moved to Rye in 1897, and Conrad died nearby in 1924. Ford died in Deauville in 1939, and Wells after the close of the Second World War. It would be absurd to pretend to comprehensiveness; they all were wanderers and wandered far afield. Instead, I have operated under the assumption that a brief period, if sufficiently examined, can adumbrate decades. The years of the Edwardians, coeval of course with Edward's reign, are 1901–1910. But that leaves us with the uneasy interval before the First World War, as well as the war itself and the several candidates for the year that starts modernity. Virginia Woolf would claim tongue in cheek that "on or about December 1910, human character changed."[7] Returning from the First World War, Robert Graves could be summarial, dispatching the past with *Goodbye to All That.* Yet as they surely knew, an era does not end with calendar-like precision. It has to be forced into form.

I have elected accordingly to focus on a single year. That focus will be blurred throughout, but it should be acknowledged. The turn of the century must have seemed consequential to them; it does so, still, to me. It is the year of Crane's death; Queen Victoria was to die six months later, in January 1901. To call the 1900 writers "Edwardians" is therefore proleptic, a convenience. Ford and Wells were beginning their careers, and certainly not as Victorians. The much older Conrad was also just starting to publish; his first book, *Almayer's Folly*, appeared in 1895. James was embarking on the period of his major novels; to greet the new era, he shaved off his beard. England was unrivaled in security and power. That solid conviction of substance, however, was being tested by the Boer War. In politics as well as painting, things were in obvious flux; morals and mores were everywhere called to account. As Yeats would put it, after the centennial's apocalypse had failed to come to pass, "everybody got down off his stilts; henceforth nobody drank absinthe with his black coffee; nobody went mad; nobody committed suicide; nobody joined the Catholic Church; or if they did I have forgotten."[8]

In 1900 these figures among others attained the age of thirty-five: King George V, Rudyard Kipling, and Yeats himself. John Ruskin, Arthur Sullivan, and Oscar Wilde were among those who died. *The Daily Express* and *The Oxford Book of English Verse* appeared, as did *Lord Jim* and Wells's *Love and Mr. Lewisham*. It was the year of the Relief of Mafeking as well as the Boxer Rebellion; it saw the first Zeppelin flight, the Central London Railway —the "tuppenny tube"—and the announcement of the Commonwealth of Australia as well as quantum theory. Next year Roger Fry, Ramsay MacDonald, Beatrix Potter, and H. G. Wells turned thirty-five; Richard D'Oyly Carte and Kate Greenaway died. That year produced the publication of Hegelian cosmology and Kipling's *Kim*; Edward VII acceded to the throne and President William McKinley was shot. In 1902 the Boer War ended and Cecil Rhodes died; the Aswan Dam was built, as were the

Old Bailey and Deptford Town Hall. The *Just So Stories* appeared, as did *The Times Literary Supplement* and *Peter Rabbit*, "Youth" and *The Wings of the Dove*. The coronation of Edward VII took place on June 26. No prince had ever been more lengthily prepared for rule; no monarch acceded to the throne at such an advanced age —fifty-nine. John Galsworthy and Arnold Bennett turned thirty-five in 1902; Ford would not do so till 1908. The times were Janus-faced.

To pretend, however, that these men had no antecedent or subsequent careers would be as foolish as to try to be inclusive. James repeatedly demonstrates that an idea may take years to germinate; a piece of gossip or an anecdote or incident may find its artistic expression only long after the fact. So, too, with an aesthetic. Ford's enduring novel, *The Good Soldier*, appeared in 1915—but the name of its protagonist, Ashburnham, is present already in his 1900 book on the region, *The Cinque Ports*. A record of his collaboration with Conrad in that twelve-month period alone would deny continuity; *Romance* took years to complete. Nor, for that matter, did their potboiling novella, "The Nature of a Crime," find separate publication until 1924. In the year 1900 the epistolary exchange between James and Wells was sweetly polite; one can see the seeds of their later quarrel, however, in the letters of Alphonse and Gaston.

The range of acquaintance was in every instance wide, and James would never feel as close to Wells as, say, to Hugh Walpole. Conrad and Ford aside, the relations were those of friendship and not intimacy. It would give an improper perspective to picture this group as exclusive; nor did they form any sort of salon. Perhaps, though this is pure speculation, the absence of talented women accounts for the latter absence. (Or, more precisely, the talented women were kept to one side. Jean Rhys and Rebecca West, for example, are far more than mistress-muses—but they had relatively little contact with their men's workaday world. Nor had these two entered the picture as of 1900.) Certainly no woman of the beauty of Virginia and Vanessa Stephen, or of the efficiency of Alice Toklas, kept a "salon" together. Cora Crane was Crane's true consort and might have managed to do so, but after his death she withdrew. And Jessie Conrad had no use for Ford . . .

Influence is never easy to determine. And acknowledgment thereof seems rare; we tend to cover our tracks. With the exception of Ford, whose memoirs have been traditionally dismissed as fiction, these authors staked no shared claim. Jealous of their reputations—or reported on by jealous wives—they denied rather than affirmed the rumor of cohesiveness. When Wells introduced Conrad to G. B. Shaw, it nearly occasioned a duel. James looked askance at Crane's entourage and apologized on Crane's behalf to Mrs. Humphry Ward: "It's as if . . . you should find in a staid drawing-room on Beacon Hill or Washington Square or at an intimate reception at Washington a Cockney—oh, I admit of the greatest genius—but a Cockney still, costermonger from Whitechapel."[9] The conflict between Wells and James is famous, nor was Kipling often affable. Yet the fallings-out and arguments seem to me germane.

So here is no "love interest" and the consequent shared lives. Galsworthy's romance may have furnished him the tale of Bosinney and Irene, but it very nearly cost him entry to the artistic establishment; Ford records how, on the brink of the divorce action, Galsworthy was convinced that all doors would henceforth be shut. And Ford's own tangled affairs, when made public, helped occasion the rupture with Conrad. Nowhere were Conrad and James so little venturesome as in matters of propriety. Monastic in their devotion to the strict dictates of work, they expected monkishness also in their acolytes. Here the age difference applies. Wells's experiments in sexual freedom would have startled his neighbors much more than did his intellectual forays; that Cora was not Crane's legal wife and may have joined him from a whorehouse would scarcely, had James known it, have increased his regard. We are denied therefore—except as a collaborative title—the whole range of "romance."

Yet perspective does imply selection, and selection an exclusiveness; the nameless interlocutor goes cruelly ignored because he has no name. Nor is the "person from Porlock" fondly remembered. He interrupted Coleridge in the act of composition. Had he not knocked on the door, the poet could have continued to function as a solitary, and we could continue to share *Kubla Khan*. The literary historian in this sense must create a retrospective party. When Thoreau goes walking with Emerson or takes tea at Margaret Fuller's, it becomes—in hindsight—an event. If Emerson or Fuller were not in themselves personages, Thoreau would simply have gone for a stroll or a drink. This has to do with the prospect of influence, and that of valuative time. It is reasonable to assume that the youthful Crane would have paid intense attention to his older and revered compatriot—and the quality of such association makes the question of quantity moot.

The English house is hedged. It hides behind a thick green wall. This is not for tax purposes, as with the French, where shabby exterior maintenance can keep a palace private. Nor is it built along the model of a court-yard, as in those hot countries where a family hunts shade. Rather, the privacy here suggests a public reticence, a keeping to oneself. This may be predicated on the fear of overcrowding; it makes of each house a miniature island with garden walls acting as shore.

But though a man's home is his castle, it need not be fortified. The most casual of encounters still yields the feel of trust; a house requires no lock. Village greens and public footpaths abound. People gather to gossip at church or while shopping; the postman knows who waits behind each door. The milkman still brings milk down every entrance pathway, and the dustman wears clean clothes. James may have been no hero to his valet, Burgess Noakes, but Noakes would not betray this to the folk of Rye. Homes are restored and not razed. "What was good enough for Granddad is good enough for me" seems an actual mode of management. Things last. There are places in the world, of course, where the twentieth century has made fewer inroads—but these are by and large those places that the nineteenth or the eighteenth did not alter either. Kent and East Sussex are not "backward"; they have managed to maintain a sense of the present past.

Half a dozen houses with no common vista can have gateways giving on common land. Those folk who live a guarded life behind the privet hedge or who prune their holly so that it seems impenetrable will nonetheless grow garrulous at teatime or in pubs. The English keep a very convivial solitude. And I like to think of our five authors as adjacent on a green. Their dwellings are dissimilar in size and shape and trim. Some are "Antient," some distinguished, and one of them is new. They live alone or pretend to be married, or are married and have children; the marriages are solid or about to crack. These neighbors like to walk and ride on bicycles and dogcarts; they covet motorcars. They wear, at times, outlandish gear; one of them looks like a cowboy, and one of them looks like a priest. When they meet on the green in the evening's last light, they talk of money matters, of great schemes for editions and their canny friends in London who do well. . . .

If they argue over novels, it has to do with purpose at least as much as style. "To walk down Piccadilly with a poppy or a lily" has hitherto been a privilege reserved for poets—or, more fairly, poetasters. Those who publish novels have "worked at the writing trade." But an American and a Polish aesthete who each have been to France have brought back and translated notions of the dignity inherent in the genre. They revise. One of them will go so far as to bring out an edition—emended and selected, prefaced at length—of the books he wishes to preserve. It is an elaborate procedure, and it sets a standard of high seriousness. Others complain. All things are mutable, they say, and mankind's in the making; why dignify one's impulse and render it so earnest; why shouldn't art be play? Or, more important, why should it not partake of the quotidian and passing issue: news?

They are prodigious workers, all of them; they do not need to shop or cook or wash the children's clothes. They have gardeners. They wake and settle at their desks; they work while they eat their suppers and when they entertain. If deadlines impinge—and they seem to, regularly—they will write for half the night. They drink watered whiskey or fruit juice or *vin ordinaire*. They complain of various ailments, but the one who makes no such complaint is the first and the youngest to die. They are conscious, I assume, of what peculiar birds they seem in their foreign plumage to the locals on the green. But this does not inhibit them; if anything, they foster the effect. They drawl and carry pistols and flourish their umbrellas or their walking sticks. They will change the face of fiction in our time.

If all this seems a bit far-fetched, why, then, so were our authors. One the son of a cricketer brought up belowstairs to herald this leveling age; one a Polish aristocrat who became a sailor and took to writing novels while becalmed in the Far East; one a man who changed his name so that the last repeats the first, and changed his affectations as often as he did his publisher; two Americans who died abroad with no college educations, who are today requir-ed reading in colleges at home—they make an improba-ble group. There is no record of their having shared a roof at once. They did not exchange beds. They did not always agree, and their disagreements were fierce. The "friendly voice" insisting in this chapter's epigraph is Ford's. "It was not an argument," says Conrad. "But I submitted at once." He then elaborates:

> You perceive the force of a word. He who wants to per-suade should put his trust not in the right argument, but in the right word. . . . Of course the accent must be attended to. The right accent. That's very important. The capacious lung, the thundering or the tender vocal chords. Don't talk to me of your Archimedes' lever. He was an absent-minded person with a mathematical imagi-nation. Mathematics commands all my respect, but I have no use for engines. Give me the right word and the right accent and I will move the world.[10]

" 'You know, you really must,' " is Ford addressing Conrad. The subsequent second-person address, "You per-ceive the force of a word," variously implicates both Ford and the audience—us. We join them in the room and on the page.

Conrad concerned himself rather more with behavior than place. His voyager's sense of the world suggested a code of conduct that should apply at least as much in the jungle as in town. In "Heart of Darkness," indeed, Marlow compares London's past to that of Africa's dark present—

and Conrad's fiction of those years was organized by the dream of a civilized solidarity. In *Lord Jim* he repeatedly poses the problem of what it entails to be "one of us"; Marlow wonders aloud and in several contexts why he will not "go ashore for a howl and a dance."[11] Yet James was writing of just such restraint, and the moral imperatives attendant on a stranger. His antipodes are those of Europe and America—but Milly Theale is as much an alien in Lancaster Gate as is Jim in Patusan. Crane and Wells would also take the topic of what we now might call the dislocated self. Their protagonists range back through history and forward in time machines, but the question is continual: what happens to a crowd composed of individuals—what is sacrificed, what gained?

Kipling and Wells wielded very public power, and Ford could claim in earnest—in his book on James, as elsewhere—that a first-rate piece of prose meant more to an empire than trains. Art and the economy are linked, he would insist; what keeps the hotel beds in Stratford-on-Avon occupied if not the bard who left his wife his second-best bed there? The opportunity to dine with ministers of state was neither unusual nor an occasion for publicity; writers of that time could feel—witness the Fabians —that what they had to say might matter to the nation. It is as easy to exaggerate such power in retrospect as to mourn its relative absence these days, but I think it fair to say that artists then could call themselves at least potentially acknowledged legislators. England was a literate nation; its recent prime minister, Disraeli, was himself a novelist of no small achievement and skill.

In such a circumstance, the standard of "Art for Art's Sake" was not merely *faute de mieux*; it entailed a conscious choice. Crane was famous as a journalist, but he came to Brede to write fiction. And the opposition—nowhere as manifest as in the conflict between James and Wells—has ramifications today. It will be worth considering at length and in a later chapter, but the essential argument continues. It has to do with the very nature of art, its role and function in the state, and what the writer can hope to accomplish. To take a commercial example, *What Maisie Knew* sold fewer copies in its first year of publication than *The Time Machine* in an average month; eighty years later, the figures are no doubt reversed. That literary fortune need not be coeval with literary merit is no news. The point here is the conscious—and eloquently argued—clash of aesthetics: whom should one take for one's audience, and to what purpose, and how? From the much later vantage of his autobiography, Wells recalls:

> I find myself worrying round various talks and discussions I had with Henry James a third of a century ago. He was a very important figure in the literary world of that time and a shrewd and penetrating critic of the technique by which he lived. He liked me and he found my work respectable enough to be greatly distressed about it. I bothered him and he bothered me. We were at cross purposes based . . . on very fundamental differences, not only of temperament but training. He had no idea of the possible use of the novel as a help to conduct. His mind had turned away from any such idea. From his point of view there were not so much "novels" as The Novel, and it was a very high and important achievement. He thought of it as an Art Form and of novelists as artists of a very special and exalted type. He was concerned about their greatness and repute. He saw us all as Masters or would-be Masters, little Masters and great Masters, and he was plainly sorry that "Cher Maître" was not an English expression. One could not be in a room with him for ten minutes without realizing the importance he attached to the dignity of this art of his. I was by nature and education unsympathetic with this mental disposition. But I

was disposed to regard a novel as about as much an art form as a market place or a boulevard. It had not even necessarily to get anywhere. You went by it on your various occasions.[12]

A corollary attaches here, having to do with the writer as businessman. Even James, the most mandarin of authors, felt the shoe pinch and wrote with the high hope of profit. His early journalism, his ill-fated foray into the theater, his lecture tours all concerned earning a living by art. Ford and Conrad in their collaborative efforts tried to out-Stevenson Stevenson and corner the *Treasure Island* market; Crane worked to keep the creditors at bay. This is a partial explanation, perhaps, of what will be a constant riddle in these pages: how professionals who wrote so well could also write so poorly. The most ardent champion of Crane, Ford, and Wells must give a large proportion of their output the alms of oblivion; they composed in a hurry and too much. This is surprising not so much by contrast to their predecessors or contemporaries as to the standard that Ford himself set, proclaiming what Flaubert had claimed a generation earlier: every word must count.

The collaborations provide the clearest example of this. No serious reader can take the fragment of *The Ghost* seriously, nor does *The Inheritors*—though better by some distance than its press—merit sustained attention. But the process of collaboration does. Since it puts the theory of colleagueship to the test of practice, it will take stage center in this book. James's offer to act as Well's reader seems genuine enough, as was Crane's proposition to Conrad. And the labors shared by Ford and Conrad bore real fruit. Here the riddle is most pressing, since the answer entails a secret of growth: how could the author of *Romance* proceed to write *Nostromo*; how could the author of *The Last Post* have earlier produced so slight a thing as "The Nature of a Crime"? Even granted a degree of self-delusion or plain propaganda, the letters of those years express conviction: what they were doing was worth it, and worth doing well. An author's work is always more like his own other work than that of anyone else—but such disparity is notable: the worst stands catercorner to the best. What resulted, clearly, was a faith in process—almost despite the result.

Whatever lapses occurred, moreover, the aspiration remained. Work was a constant; they worked when ordered to rest. Crane was writing while on his deathbed; so was Wells (even if, in *The Mind at the End of Its Tether*, he countermanded much he had written before). Ford tipped his cap to Hokusai and called himself an "old man mad about writing." His *The March of Literature* is in its own way as ambitious, massive, and idiosyncratic an undertaking as Wells's *The Outline of History*. The range astonishes; they wrote of politics and science, wrote journalism and verse. The notion that a man might be learned in more than one discipline seemed plausible then still; it encouraged our authors to write about anything under the sun.

Such dexterity would not be confined to the page. Nineteen hundred was a time when conversation flourished, and though we may take the testimonials with a grain of salt, there are several who attest the brilliance of their talk. Conrad was apparently rapid in speech if not composition; the written page denies inflection and the support of gesture. James's dictation posits a degree of rhetorical assurance that we have largely lost. Ford, too, dictated *The Good Soldier*, and no matter how often reworked on the page, these books bear witness to their origins in speech. The characters are fluent also. Marlow and Dowell have the kind of narrative ease that bespeaks a long habit of fireside discourse—as well as the conviction that some friend will sit and listen. What Marlow most wanted of Kurtz was the chance to have a talk, and Christopher Tietjens thinks of love as lifelong conversation; when the seduction is over, one settles down to chat. Even George Ponderevo, of Wells's *Tono-Bungay*—who protests himself a self-taught man of little language—can express himself expressively. When their characters went incoherent, the Edwardians intended this to signal the disrupted coherence of things.

For everyone knew everyone, it seems. Here, from Ada Galsworthy's notebook, is a list of the people the Galsworthys met:

> During the years 1905 to 1910, the literary men and others with whom J. G. most associated were: Joseph Conrad, Edward Garnett, Ford Madox Hueffer, E. V. Lucas, W. H. Hudson, Granville Barker, Gilbert Murray, J. M. Barrie, William Archer, G. B. Shaw, John Masefield, R. A. Scott-James, A. J. Legge, C.F.G. Masterman, Gilbert Cannan, A. Sutro, Max Beerbohm, Arnold Bennett, H. G. Wells (last 2 slightly) Laurence Housman, H. W. Nevinson, H. W. Massingham, A. J. Hobson, W. J. Locke, H. Vachell, Anthony Hope, A.E.W. Mason, Ed. Gosse, Sidney Colvin, J. W. Hills, Charles Roden Buxton, Arthur Ponsonby, A. Birrell, Lord Crewe, Winston Churchill, Charles Trevelyan (last 4 slightly).[13]

That constant keeping up to the mark could not have failed to fire ambition. And one way to read the novels is with reference to such collegiality. It is possible to argue, for instance, that a dominant impulse in *Lord Jim* and *The Good Soldier* is precisely to find an attentive critical ear, an astute yet merciful friend. Marlow tells his tales in need, and James's confidantes are defined as listeners. A deep purpose of art has always been the ratification of bonds; the singer and his audience grow akin. To the degree that a novel is an expression of society, it establishes as well as expresses that society. And books as disparate as *Kim* and *The Ambassadors* have in common some notion of a commonweal, of a place (whether civilized or wild) where one's strange self need not feel further estranged.

A final cautionary note. The temptation for a novelist to reinvent these folk is considerable. They dressed each other up often enough in fictive guise to justify our doing so once more. Ventures as various as David Hughes's *The Man Who Invented Tomorrow*, or Nicholas Meyer's film *Time After Time* attest the present attraction of Wells. A television serial took the Forsytes for its text, and Conrad and James reach wide-screen audiences now. If Kurtz can be a Green Beret captain gone mad in Vietnam (as in *Apocalypse Now*), why couldn't Marlow's interlocutors—those silent friends who hear him out in "Heart of Darkness"—be Crane, Ford, James, and Wells? It would be very much in Ford's mode to create a colloquy in which these five play croquet—till Crane removes his cap and brandishes his mallet and takes off after imagined Indians on James's gelding grazing nearby. He could meet Mark Twain over the hill and Bret Harte in the valley; he could rear at Kipling's automobile and pace the jogging Galsworthy and pick a nosegay that the naturalist Hudson would identify. He could gallop past a Blue Hotel, beneath a Yellow Sky. . . .

For want of horses, at one point, a projected collaborative effort between Crane and Conrad failed. The former had the notion—as did James, of course—that the theater was the road to riches. All they had to do, Crane urged the skeptical Conrad, was have a hero and heroine gallop to stage center on a pair of dying ponies, then have the two jump clear and watch the desert sunset till the curtain falls. Conrad pointed out that the necessary stable full of ponies to be sacrificed would cut into their profit margin; he declined:

> I would only be a hindrance to you—I am afraid. And it seems presumptuous of me to think of helping you. You want no help. I have a perfect confidence in your power —and why should you share with me what then may be of profit and fame in the accomplished task?[14]

Conrad's self-deprecatory *politesse* is but another way of showing that he deprecates the play. And the evasion of his letters could easily be caught in speech: a quick twist of the moustache points, that half-smile to hide refusal, the tongue flicking out to lick lips. They would have been drinking Château Pavie; Lafite this year costs twenty pounds a case. They would be eating oysters because one or the other had just made a sale. . . . It is tempting to embroider, or to be—as Ford would argue—faithful to the impression if not the picayune fact.

But to the best of my knowledge and research, nothing in what follows is conjectural. There is much charm and interest in those biographies that paint the sunset of May 23, 1900, in a splendid spectrum that we otherwise would fail to see, or that evoke the feel of leather and a horse's sweating flanks. But these men have done so by themselves, and sufficiently; there will be no flashing eyes or satisfying clink of silver on plate unless in quotation or as direct report. In addition to the reasons for *Group Portrait* adduced above, there remains this last and best: I love to read these novelists, and hope that others will.

II.

Stephen Crane in England

Along a winding, white Road which led toward the East, a large number of Travellers proceeded with huge Manuscripts under their Arms. Some passed along with shrinking Timidity; Others held their Heads so high that They stumbled at every Step. At intervals, certain Men would rush from the Woods at the Roadside and beat the Travellers unmercifully.

> —STEPHEN CRANE, "In the Country of Rhymers and Writers," 1892

II.
Stephen Crane
in England

On December 28, 1899, the tenants of Brede Place put on a play at the Brede schoolhouse. It was called *The Ghost*, conceived of as an entertainment for the locals and as a celebration. It has a collective authorship —attested on the title page—unequaled in our time. Few manuscript pages survive, but the program of *The Ghost* asserts that it is written by Mr. Henry James, Mr. Robert Barr, Mr. George Gissing, Mr. Rider Haggard, Mr. Joseph Conrad, Mr. H. B. Marriott-Watson, Mr. H. G. Wells, Mr. Edwin Pugh, Mr. A.E.W. Mason, and Mr. Stephen Crane.

This last named was the prime mover. It was his place, his party and idea. He and Cora occupied the manor house as if to the manor born—though Crane hailed from Newark, New Jersey, and Cora covered her tracks. She had good reason to: the track had taken her from "hostess" in a nightclub in Jacksonville, Florida, the Hotel de Dream; there, she first met Crane. Her previous husband refused a divorce, and she called herself Mrs. Crane out of a greater regard for convention than truth. They came to England together in 1897 and settled in Oxted; two years later they moved out to Brede. When the glad, brief dream was done, Cora would return to Jacksonville, where by 1902 she had built and was operating a whorehouse called The Court.

But Brede Place was a very different proposition, a four-teenth-century structure built to last. It stands there still: a vast arrangement of stone and oak, with mullioned, leaded windows giving out on windswept land. Moreton Frewen owned the house and leased it to the Cranes for a nominal sum; it was in disrepair. William the Conqueror landed nearby, and Brede was an outpost of Normandy for 363 years. Crane, describing it in "The Squire's Madness" and *The O'Ruddy*, gave it its fair share of ghosts; his letters are alive with pride in such down-at-the-heels grandeur. As "The Ghost" intones in his opening speech, "It is difficult to be a ghost here. I would like to have an easier place. Tourists come here and they never give me a penny although I had my last pipe of 'baccy two hundred years ago and I drank my last pint of bitter in 1531 . . ."[1]

Within this damp establishment, drinking flat ale, chain-smoking and writing in a little room over the porch, Crane spent his final year. A visitor, Karl Harriman, declared that Brede Place killed him with its lack of proper drainage and its improper fiscal drains. They enter-tained enormously. Crane called his hangers-on "lice," but he liked to be labeled Baron or Duke and he provisioned the house as only a wide-eyed, wildly improvident for-eigner might. If his American callers were "Indians," he received them in his notion of a squire's style. His morning ride in the hundred-acre "little park" was on one of two white horses; he had, according to Ford, "A barrell of beer and a baron of beef . . . waiting in the rear hall for every hobo that might pass that way. The house was a nightmare of misplaced hospitality, of lugubrious dissipation in which Crane himself had no part. Grub Street and Greenwich Village did."[2]

To a war correspondent and survivor of shipwrecks, however, such company and tribulation would not have seemed severe. Crane paid no attention to expense or to his wasting health. He was almost compulsively prodigal, and defiant if called to account. Robert Louis Stevenson, that earlier consumptive Crane so scorned, had long prolonged his life by exercise in a fine climate; when he died, after fourteen years in the South Seas, it was not of tuberculosis. Whether the vapors of Brede Place were fatal or not, Crane breathed them in delightedly; the Christmas Party modulated into a New Year's celebration. H. G. Wells describes the occasion at length:

. . . I remember very vividly a marvellous Christmas Party in which Jane and I participated. We were urged to come over and, in a postscript, to bring any bedding and blankets we could spare. We arrived in a heaped-up Sandgate cab, rather in advance of the guests from London. We were given a room over the main gateway in which there was a portcullis and an owl's nest, but at least we got a room. Nobody else did—because although some thirty or forty invitations had been issued, there were not as a matter of fact more than three or four bedrooms available. One of them however was large and its normal furniture had been supplemented by a number of hired truckle-beds and christened the Girls' Dormitory, and in the attic an array of shake-downs was provided for the men. Husbands and wives were torn apart.

Later on we realized that the sanitary equipment of Brede House dated from the seventeenth century, an interesting historical detail, and such as there was indoors, was accessible only through the Girls' Dormitory. Consequently the wintry countryside next morning was dotted with wandering, melancholy, preoccupied, men guests.

Anyhow there were good open fires in the great fire-places and I remember that party as an extraordinary lark—but shot, at the close, with red intimations of a coming tragedy. We danced in the big oak-panelled room downstairs, lit by candles stuck upon iron sconces that Cora Crane had improvised with the help of the Brede blacksmith. Unfortunately she had not improvised grease guards and after a time everybody's back showed a patch of composite candle-wax, like the flash on the coat of a Welsh Fusilier. When we were not dancing or romping we were waxing the floor or rehearsing a play vamped up by A.E.W. Mason, Crane, myself and others. It was a ghost play, and very allusive and fragmentary, and we gave it in the School Room at Brede. It amused its authors and cast vastly. What the Brede people made of it is not on record.[3]

No amount of allusive interlinears can turn *The Ghost* into more than mere farce; it is not something the authors took seriously. Nor need the reader. Crane himself was horrified at the thought that critics might; he downplayed the play. When Moreton Frewen asked for a copy of the text so as to show it in London, Crane wrote him on New Year's Day:

> . . . I am desolated by your request because I fear it is the result of a misunderstanding. It is true that we gave a play in the village school house but the whole thing was a mere idle string of rubbish made to entertain the villagers and with music frankly stolen from very venerable comic operas such as "The Mikado" and "Pinafore." The whole business was really beneath contempt to serious people and it would be inconsiderate, even unkind, of me to send it to you. The names of the authors was more of a joke than anything. Still, we made it genuine by causing all these men to write a mere word or phrase—such as

"It's cold" or, in fact anything at all—and in this way we arranged this rather historic little program. Allow me to wish you a very fine shining 1900.[4]

Conrad wrote rather more than "It's cold"; his single contribution was "This is a jolly cold world." Someone else added the following: "He died of an indignity caught in running after his hat down Piccadilly." So perhaps the pervading chill of the manor—there was a sizable snowstorm on December 29—invaded the dramatic weather also. Wells offered his Doctor Moreau for the cast of characters, and Henry James's Peter Quint became the son of Doctor Moreau. The whole was a pastiche. A final chorus contains such less than haunting lyrics as:

I've had more trouble than a heap of Sussex men,
Don't you tell, my Brede Hill Belle,
And I save all the money the silly tourists spend,
For my Belle, Brede Hill Belle.
If I try hard to drop her and to get a maid more gay,
Then she says, "Oh my honey not today,
Don't you be a foolish ghost,
You are sure to love *me* most,"
Then she sighs, and she cries, Oh![5]

But "this distinguished rabble" (as Crane called it in a letter to H. B. Marriott-Watson soliciting that author's contribution) could not well go unnoticed. *The Manchester Guardian*, on January 13, 1900, averred that "a remarkable piece of literary patchwork has lately been allowed to waste its sweetness on the Sussex air. This is a play which has been written for an amateur performance by a string of our most popular novelists. . . . One is deeply sorry that it is not to be published."[6] And, according to the local newspaper accounts, the play was a success. "The songs, most of which were encored, were tastefully accompanied on the piano by Mrs. H. G. Wells. At the close of the performance a vote of thanks to the performers . . . was carried by acclamation. The audience sang, 'For they are jolly good people,' the original word being changed in consideration of the ladies among those acting."[7]

What's clear about the enterprise is its great good humor, and the sense of celebration the Cranes carried with them everywhere. Crane was the youngest of the group; his revelry was licensed till the end. Forty-five years later, A.E.W. Mason—who had had some theater experience and therefore played "The Ghost"—recalled the occasion as follows:

> I know that I was given a room to myself but warned not to open, except very cautiously, two great doors which enclosed one side of it. There was no electric light and naturally enough I opened very carefully the two doors. I found that if I had taken one step forward, I should have stepped down about thirty feet into the chapel, this being the private pew or box of the owners of the house. We had, I remember, rushes on the floor instead of carpets, and there were other disadvantages which meant nothing to us, for we were all of us young.[8]

And Edith Ritchie Jones, who played one of "the three little maids from Rye," announced as late as 1954 that "I have never known two people more deeply in love with one another than were Stephen and Cora. Their sweetness and consideration each for the other were touching and charming. . . . Cora asked Stephen if he had enjoyed the party and he said yes, every bit of it."[9]

Half a century can help eradicate the chill, and parties may improve in retrospect. But Wells in the thirties, Mason in the forties, and Edith Ritchie Jones in the fifties all agree with the hot-off-the-presses accounts: they had fun. Brede Place was a fine place to visit, its ghosts most amiable, and its hosts most kind. Crane was an impresario but not, it seems, self-serving; his sense of fraternity may have derived from something like a correspondent's code. He tells of having filed dispatches in the Cuban War for a mortally wounded colleague, and tales of camaraderie abound. If he traveled with a pack, it was not always automatically at the head thereof.

Yet fame has its own inertia—and he would be, increasingly, singled out for praise. If headlines blazoned "Stephen Crane Safe" after the *Commodore* disaster, that was not Crane's problem; he had been one among many when in "The Open Boat." There is something studied, perhaps, about that open-handed, shirt-off-my-back swagger of the American who came to camp in a great ancient house in Sussex—but the open-handedness was real. Ford says:

> Crane was the most beautiful spirit I have ever known. He was small, frail, energetic, at times virulent. He was full of fantasies and fantasticisms. He would fly at and deny every statement before it was out of your mouth. He wore breeches, riding leggings, spurs, a cowboy's shirt and there was always a gun near him in the mediaeval building that he inhabited seven miles from Winchelsea. In that ancient edifice he would swat flies with precision and satisfaction with the bead-sight of his gun . . .[10]

He supported this establishment on credit, however, owing even for the firewood they burned. The papers made much of the fact that Crane paid the theatrical expenses himself, providing the people of Brede with free Christmas entertainment. If so, it was one of the few debts he honored; the butcher, baker, and candlestick-maker may have come to the performance in order to collect. It is a scene straight from Smollett or Fielding—the artful gentlemen declaiming, the ladies capering, the snowstorm and wassail, then the young phthisic hero so pale in evening clothes. . . .

And he played the squire role to excess; at the end of

the party, Crane collapsed. Wells—who himself had contracted tuberculosis when young and had moved to Sandgate for reasons of his health—reports:

> In the night after the play Mrs. Crane came to us. He had had a haemorrhage from his lungs and he had tried to conceal it from her. He "didn't want anyone to bother." Would I help get a doctor?
>
> There was a bicycle in the place and my last clear memory of that fantastic Brede House party is riding out of the cold skirts of a wintry night into a drizzling dawn along a wet road to call up a doctor in Rye.[11]

Those "red intimations of a coming tragedy" would fade; Crane had resilience. He recovered quickly from this first attack. Edith Ritchie left the house party convinced all would be well. And when Ford came to call, on January 2, Crane was healthy enough to receive him—though not for the first minutes, since he seems to have mistaken Ford for the bailiff. One letter to Pinker implores discretion in money matters, since the postman is also his grocer. So he would hide from friends as well as bill collectors the truth of straitened circumstances. The disease itself, with its relapses and remissions and bouts of febrile energy, may have contributed here. It is difficult to know at what point Crane gave up. He and Cora would engage, for the final six months of his life, in an ever more desperate fiction as to the facts of his health. He produced a last will and testament only shortly before departing for a sanatorium in Germany. As Wells puts it, "He did his utmost to conceal his symptoms and get on with his dying."

The degree of Crane's self-awareness is impossible to determine. His letters are by and large of the hale-fellow-well-met-variety, but he does not seem deluded. He knew he was terribly ill. And he had no use for doctors or expressed solicitude; he rejected all offers of help. One friend received this warning: "Please have the kindness to keep your mouth shut about my health in front of Mrs. Crane hereafter. She can do nothing for me and I am too old to be nursed. It's all up with me but I will not have her scared. For some funny woman's reason she likes me. Mind this."[12]

The image of the *poète maudit*, half in love with easeful death, is clearly one that compelled John Berryman in his biography of Crane. And that view had contemporary currency. Willa Cather wrote, "He had the precocity of those doomed to die in youth. I am convinced that when I met him he had a vague premonition of the shortness of his working day, and in the heart of the man there was that which said, 'That thou doest, do quickly.' "[13] He was often compared to Edgar Allan Poe and even called a later incarnation; he would expose himself repeatedly to danger, making mortality his subject. This descriptive passage, from "An Episode of War," is characteristic: a lieutenant is wounded. The wound confers a kind of dignity in apartness, the mark of one about to die and whom the survivors revere:

> One timidly presented his shoulder and asked the lieutenant if he cared to lean upon it, but the latter waved him away mournfully. He wore the look of one who knows he is the victim of a terrible disease and understands his helplessness. He again stared over the breastwork at the forest, and then, turning, went slowly rearward. He held his right wrist tenderly in his left hand as if the wounded arm was made of very brittle glass.
>
> And the men in silence stared at the wood, then at the departing lieutenant; then at the wood, then at the lieutenant.[14]

In "The Veteran," as if to dispel any lingering question of Henry Fleming's bravery, Crane gives us "the youth" of *The Red Badge of Courage* when confronting death. He is now a grandfather and admired by all; he cheerfully confesses that he had known cowardice while at Chancellorsville. But he alone keeps his presence of mind during a barn-burning, rescuing the animals. And he chooses to return for "two colts in the box-stalls at the back of the barn," though "it's sure death." The barn becomes a crucible—and death, apotheosis:

> When the roof fell in, a great funnel of smoke swarmed towards the sky, as if the old man's mighty spirit, released from its body—a little bottle—had swelled like the genie of fable. The smoke was tinted rose-hue from the flames, and perhaps the unutterable midnights of the universe will have no power to daunt the color of this soul.[15]

The guilt of the survivor that informs this stance is characteristic of those American authors who missed the Civil War. The youngest of fourteen children, Crane lost his father at age eight and his mother at nineteen. Too young of course to have had experience of the Civil War (Crane was born in 1871), his imaginative reconstruction thereof is powered by a sense of loss. Henry Fleming in *The Red Badge* is at the edge of action only, a pampered child. The pale cast of thought has sicklied him—yet conscience can make heroes of us all. The typical Crane hero witnesses an action before he avoids or enters it. He must grow into "the veteran." But the avoidance, in biographical terms, was of disease, not death. The recklessness so characteristic of Crane—the devil-may-care bravery that is the stuff of anecdote—seems an elected stance. It is the attitude of one who nerves and schools himself to manhood, as if war (and, at its farthest limit, suicide) were an initiation rite.

If Poe preceded him, Hemingway would follow. The latter's motto of "grace under pressure" applies in retrospect. Hemingway would claim to have liberated Paris, drinking champagne in the cafés while General Leclerc and the regular troops advanced. Crane, earlier, did much the same. In Puerto Rico he walked alone into the village of Juana Diaz. According to Richard Harding Davis, "His khaki suit, slouched hat and leggings were all that was needed to drive the first man he saw, or rather the man who first saw him, back upon the town in disorderly retreat. . . ."[16] So when the troops arrived, the correspondent had taken the town. And the heroism of his behavior under fire, or his endurance when shipwrecked, his drinking bouts and whoring and all-night poker games—these are the meat and drink of legend. It is as if he felt himself, the watcher, watched. The extent to which witting self-destruction is implicit in such fascination with destruction is of course conjectural, but it surprised no one of his acquaintance that Crane died young.

This might well have formed a basis for friendship with Henry James. James, too, was afflicted by the war, although as someone old enough to have fought. His short story "Owen Wingrave" depicts a pacifist, heroic in spite of himself and not unlike the subsequent Henry Fleming. In James's fiction of these years the image of doomed youth recurs. *The Sacred Fount* describes a country house party that may have been suggested by the celebration at Brede—though James could have drawn on his fund of experience for five hundred other such parties. More centrally, Mrs. Brissenden flourishes at the expense of her much younger husband—as, it appeared, did Cora. As Leon Edel suggests, the figure of the gifted youth too fragile for this world "was a very old theme with James," as was "the way in which men and women prey on one another." And Edel then makes the identification explicit. "During the first months of the new year, when Crane was ill most of the time, Henry James wrote *The Sacred Fount*. It may have derived some of its poignancy from the vision

the novelist had of the way in which Crane was visibly
dying while Cora thrived, seemingly unaware of the tragedy being lived out under her roof."[17]

James was not so forgiving of Cora's eccentricities as
were her English neighbors; he was readily able to distinguish Stephen's solid background from Cora's mysterious
past. Or, possibly, license would be granted to the artist
—whereas his companion should observe a strict decorum.
And in the final months at Brede, Cora lost control. The
money extracted from Pinker was squandered on restoration work; specialists were summoned from London with
much fanfare and to no avail; the expedition to Badenweiler was too long postponed to be of any real use. The
concluding phrase of Crane's "The Squire's Madness" must
have been bitter to Cora: "It is your wife who is mad.
Mad as a Hatter!"[18] Yet James sent fifty pounds and
requested that Cora "dedicate it to whatever service it
might best render my stricken friend. It meagerly represents my tender benediction to him."[19]

One must tread lightly here. The burden of Edel's analysis of friendship between James and Crane is that there
was in fact little. Several of the morning canters between
Brede Place and Lamb House may well have been
invented, nor does James seem likely to have—according
to the story—dropped by unannounced with guests by the
carriageful. He did send one note saying he'd missed
them on the road, but Brede Place with its shabby furnish-
ings, its complement of drunks and dabblers, was not to
his taste. The most famous of the anecdotes is possibly
embroidered. Thomas Beer, Crane's first biographer, offers
it as follows:

> To this matrix of a pleasant evening were suddenly added
> a nobleman then in alliance with a lady never certain as
> to her nationality, understood to be the honored subject
> of verses in "The Yellow Book" and reputed chaste

though seldom sober. The party came back to Mr. Gris-
wold's rooms in London and Madame Zipango—(the
name is certainly international)—was imitating Yvette
Guilbert when Henry James appeared to pay his young
compatriot a call. The correct and the incorrect swam together in a frightful collision. Crane withdrew the elderly
novelist to a corner and talked style until the fantastic
woman poured champagne in the top hat of Henry James.
Her noble lover had gone to sleep . . . The wretched host
of this group was too young and too frightened to do anything preventive and Crane, coldly tactful, got the hand-
some creature out of the hotel, then came back to aid in
the restoration of the abused hat.[20]

For the literary critic, the operative phrase here is that
the two "talked style." What's strange about the occasion
is that Crane was not amused. It's the sort of thing he
would have engaged in or applauded elsewhere—the
irreverence for propriety that had been his stock-in-trade.
And the story of James's having shared his manuscripts
with Crane also merits discussion. After a night of poker,
according to Beer, Crane led a group of unshaven friends
to Rye and intended to call on James. They refreshed
themselves at the Mermaid Tavern, a few doors and a very
far cry down the street from Lamb House. It is a fabled
drinker's haunt and must have been a mote in James's
middle distance. . . .

When told that Lamb House was not open to strangers,
Crane offered to fight his informant. Then he announced
that James had sent him manuscripts, and he and his companions were there with the examined texts. Once again
we may well hold the tale to be apocryphal. Yet the
important point is that Crane (or, at a remove, Beer)
would have proposed such a fiction. He could certainly
have introduced himself as "Baron" Brede or insisted on
James as his American uncle. He could have told any

number of tales in order to convince his tavern acquaintance of his welcome at Lamb House, and that he'd been
persona grata there before. And therefore his explanation
is significant, whether literally or metaphorically: he had
journeyed to talk about prose.

James had many degrees and gradations of acquaintance. His politeness to Stephen and Cora might have
been, at the beginning, routine. And his concluding note
to Cora was more than routinely unkind; he would not, he
announced, be at home. But the reports of their association are not mere fantasy, and Edel's denial should be
read more as corrective than correction. The following
passage in Ford seems, as with so much else in his memoirs, true to the feel of the whole. It bears close reading:

> The final tragedy of poor Steevie did not find him want-
> ing. It was tragedy. The sunlight fell blighted into that
> hollow, the spectres waved their draped arms of mist, the
> parasites howled and belched on the banks of Brede.
> That was horrible. But much more horrible was the sight
> of Crane at his labours. They took place in a room in the
> centre bar of the E of the Place, over the arched entry.
> Here Crane would sit writing, hour after hour and day
> after day, racked with the anxiety that he would not be
> able to keep going with his pen alone all that fantastic
> crew. His writing was tiny; he used great sheets of
> paper. To see him begin at the top of the sheet with his
> tiny words was agonizing; to see him finish a page filled
> you with concern. It meant the beginning of one more
> page, and so till his death. Death came slowly, but Brede
> was a death-trap to the tuberculous.
>
> Then James' agonies began. He suffered infinitely for
> the dying boy. I would walk with him for hours over the
> marsh trying to divert his thoughts. But he would talk on
> and on. He was forever considering devices for Crane's
> comfort. Once he telegraphed to Wanamaker's for a
> whole collection of New England delicacies from pump-

kin pie to apple butter and sausage meat and clams and
soft shell crabs and minced meat and . . . everything
thinkable, so that the poor lad should know once more
and finally those fierce joys. Then new perplexities devas-
tated him. Perhaps the taste of those far off eats might
cause Steevie to be homesick and so hasten his end.
James wavered backwards and forwards between the
alternatives beneath the grey walls of Rye Town. He was
not himself for many days after Crane's death.[21]

There is manifest hyperbole here. The image of
"spectres" waving "their draped arms of mist" is standard
late Gothic, not a statement of fact. The parasites who
"howled and belched on the banks of Brede" may be a
description of Crane's "Indians," but it is written for effect
and not as reportage. I doubt Ford walked "for hours"
with James and doubt that he watched Crane write "day
after day." Nor, as the extant manuscripts attest, was
Crane's script tiny or his paper enormous. I have been
unable to retrieve a transcript of the telegram James sent
to Wanamaker's or the filled order form.

Yet the "impression" seems sincere; so does Ford's
reportage as to James's grief and dilemma. It would be a
strange piece of recollection if it had no basis whatsoever
in fact, and wasteful ingenuity. The name and number of
New England delicacies might be invented, but the perplexity that Ford describes is quintessential James. The
sense of shared exile here is acute, and ambivalence as to
what home represents; if this incident is not literally true,
it should be. The protagonist of *The Wings of the Dove*,
Milly Theale, is an emblem of just such withdrawal; she
turns "her face to the wall." One can read in all of James's
prose of the period the record of a man who watches exuberance die. It is even possible that Crane, just returned
from his Cuban adventure and soldierly exploits, would
represent to James the wounded warrior—thus bringing

home to England once again the romantic catastrophe of war.

Crane knew of James's kindnesses by 1898. In answer to a broadside attack on James by Harold Frederic, and with possible reference to the Madame Zipango imbroglio, he wrote: "I agree with you that Mr. James has ridiculous traits and lately I have seen him make a holy show of himself in a situation that—on my honour—would have been simple to an ordinary man. But it seems impossible to dislike him. He is so kind to everybody. . . ."[22] And, in a letter to Sanford Bennett, which Ford claimed as "the greatest pride of my life," Crane in effect validated his witness. "You must not be offended by Mr. Hueffer's manner. He patronizes Mr. James. He patronizes Mr. Conrad. Of course he patronizes me and he will patronize Almighty God when they meet, but God will get used to it, for Hueffer is all right."[23]

Ford knew the risks he ran; often enough in his lifetime he was accused of pure invention (a strange charge for a novelist to have to disavow). But the charge has been repeated more or less continually since his death, and the defense should therefore also be repeated. The image of Ford as a bloated boaster persists; he has been served less well in other authors' memoirs than he served them in his own. And since he is a principal witness in *Group Portrait*, it is appropriate early on to establish his veracity. Even his biographers (most notably Arthur Mizener in *The Saddest Story*) grow exasperated with the thankless task of verification and the way Ford's memory modulates. He told his tale often, and it alters in the telling. No one to my knowledge has questioned H. G. Wells's account of the party at Brede, though published thirty-four years after the event; his vivid reconstruction seems unimpeachable.

But this may be a matter of style. We accept the sen-

tence quoted above as to the problems with plumbing
(". . . the wintry countryside . . . was dotted with wandering, melancholy, preoccupied, men guests"), yet discount
Ford's statement that "parasites howled and belched on
the banks. . . ." Wells said that "nobody else . . . got a
room," but A.E.W. Mason discourses at length on his private quarters and the dangerous suspended door. Wells
said that "what the Brede people made of it (*The Ghost*)
is not on record," but he was there to receive the applause
and could have read the local newspapers. These are perfectly pardonable tropes and do not undermine what
seems to be a balanced, fair-minded report. And Conrad
remembers sitting for hours in the room where Crane
would write; when *he* asserts that Crane wrote quickly,
continually, and in a cramped hand, it seems a flat statement of fact.

So Ford should be given, I think, the benefit of the
doubt. He himself explained his strategy, in his preface to
Joseph Conrad: A Personal Remembrance. Written in
1924, and completed in Bruges (where his family and the
Conrads had briefly sojourned in 1900), it anticipates his
critics. The final paragraph of the preface explains his
habitual method:

> This then is a novel, not a monograph; a portrait, not a
> narration: for what it shall prove to be worth, a work of
> art, not a compilation. It is conducted exactly along the
> lines laid down by us, both for the novel which is biogra-
> phy and for the biography which is a novel. It is the ren-
> dering of an affair intended first of all to make you see
> the subject in his scenery. It contains no documentation
> at all; for it no dates have been looked up; even all the
> quotations but two have been left unverified, coming
> from the writer's memory. It is the writer's impression of
> a writer who avowed himself impressionist. Where the
> writer's memory has proved to be at fault over a detail

afterwards out of curiosity looked up, the writer has allowed the fault to remain on the page; but as to the truth of the impression as a whole, the writer believes that no man would care—or dare—to impugn it. It was that that Joseph Conrad asked for: the task has been accomplished with the most pious scrupulosity. *For something human was to him dearer than the wealth of the Indies.*[24]

Biographers can sometimes lose the forest for the trees. The trials of tracking down material, of capturing an elusive personality can vex each sleuth until he learns to hate his man. And Ford so bullies and hectors and blandishes the reader that it's hard to resist impatience. But he has been unkindly discredited and is unjustly ignored. Eudora Welty counseled those who study Ford—and by extension all who read and write about their reading—to approach with "the response of love."[25] I can think of no better injunction and hope to follow it here.

When Ford praises Crane's ability with a spade, therefore, it is likely that Crane helped him dig. When Ford reports that Crane could kill flies with the sight of his revolver, swatting them off the table, it is probable that Crane performed some equivalent feat. When he asserts that James grieved deeply over " 'My young compatriot of genius,' " the phrase may not merit quotation marks, but the emotion persuades. Crane's library included work by James, as well as presentation copies elaborately inscribed; in the letter where he says, "I am not carnivorous about living writers," he proceeds within the paragraph to state, "I like what I know of . . . Henry James."[26]

James returned the compliment. In 1896 in his story "The Next Time," he predicted Crane's predicament. There the writer-protagonist, Ralph Limbert, keeps struggling for popular success, but is doomed by his talent to artistry and poverty. Limbert is a comic cognate for his author, not Crane; they had not as yet met. The elder American was more scrupulous and less facile. But the ironic adage that "you can't make a sow's ear of a silk purse" applies to them both; the more conscious their labors for money, the less did those labors succeed.

And though James may protest, in a letter to Cora, that he was embarrassed to have been photographed eating a doughnut from the Brede Place kitchen, he was in fact so photographed. Nor could he counterfeit the sense of waste and loss. Two days after Crane's death, he wrote Cora: "What a brutal needless extinction—what an unmitigated unredeemed catastrophe! I think of him with such a sense of possibilities & powers."[27] This last phrase is central. James was the most discerning of critics, and his interest in Crane seems to have had more to do with the latter's potential than previous achievement. He wrote to H. G. Wells: "You will have felt, as I have done, the miserable sadness of poor Crane's so precipitated and, somehow, so unnecessary extinction."[28] That day he visited the empty Brede Place and turned back, desolate.

There can be no doubt, however, of the friendship between Conrad and Crane. It was real and rich. When Crane arrived in England, he sought out the author of "The Nigger of the 'Narcissus,'" and the older yet less celebrated man was gratified. In his introduction to the Thomas Beer biography, Conrad recalls:

> It was on the ground of the authorship of that book ("The Nigger of the 'Narcissus'") that Crane wanted to meet me. Nothing could have been more flattering, than to discover that the author of "The Red Badge of Courage" appreciated my effort to present a group of men held together by a common loyalty and a common per-

plexity in a struggle not with human enemies but with
hostile conditions testing their faithfulness to the conditions of their own calling.[29]

Shared prior appreciation of the writing is an excellent
basis for friendship in writers. The private and the public
man can often be at odds, or the one can seem a stand-in
for the other. And those who read one's work *after* making
one's acquaintance may seem like partial judges, impelled
by something other than disinterest. So praise from a
friend who was previously and anyhow a friend is suspect
—as is, in the reverse instance or that of personal enmity,
criticism. I do not mean that a friend or an intimate
cannot be an important critic of one's work; the premise
of this book suggests the very opposite. But those who
"are held together by a common loyalty and a common
perplexity" when confronting "the conditions of their own
calling" can find no better starting point for solidarity than
respect. "Nothing could have been more flattering," as
Conrad writes, than to have been recognized as a kindred
artistic spirit by an admired stranger.

They met in London, at lunch. And after:

> ... the initiatory feast ... without entering formally into
> a previous agreement to remain together we went out
> and began to walk side by side in the manner of two
> tramps without home, occupation, or care for the next
> night's shelter. We certainly paid no heed to direction.
> The first thing I noticed were the Green Park railings,
> when to my remark that he had seen no war before he
> went to Greece Crane made answer: "No. But the 'Red
> Badge' is all right." I assured him that I never had
> doubted it; and, since the title of the work had been
> pronounced for the first time, feeling I must do some-
> thing to show I had read it, I said shyly: "I like your
> General." He knew at once what I was alluding to but
> said not a word. Nothing could have been more tramp-

like than our silent pacing, elbow to elbow, till after we had left Hyde Park Corner behind us, Crane uttered with his quiet earnestness, the words: "I like your young man —I can just see him."[30]

When they parted, it was with the certainty that they would meet again. "It struck me directly I left him that we had not even exchanged addresses; but I was not uneasy. Sure enough, before the month was out there arrived a post card (from Ravensbrook) asking whether he might come to see us. He came, was received as an old friend . . ." and the acquaintance deepened and endured. The letters from Crane to Conrad continue almost importunate in their requests for meetings, though Crane had company enough. "The reader will see," Conrad says, "why this is one of my most carefully preserved possessions."

RAVENSBROOK, OXTED
17 March [1899]

My Dear Conrad,

I am enclosing you a bit of MS under the supposition that you might like to keep it in remembrance of my warm and endless friendship for you. I am still hoping that you will consent to Stokes' invitation to come to the Savage on Saturday night. Cannot you endure it? Give my affectionate remembrances to Mrs. Conrad and my love to the boy.

Yours always,
Stephen Crane

P.S. You must accept says Cora—and I—our invitation to come home with me on Sat. night.[31]

Conrad did accept, and late that night they talked about collaboration on a play. *The Predecessor* was to have made a fortune for them both—at least as conceived of at Gatti's Music Hall while waiting for a train. It has less substance even than *The Ghost*, and its protagonist was also to be ghost-ridden. In order to win the girl's heart, he had to impersonate his dead "predecessor"—which scrambling of identities would cause dramatic tension. Conrad demurred:

> The scenes were to include a ranch at the foot of the Rocky Mountains, I remember, and the action I fear would have been frankly melodramatic. Crane insisted that one of the situations should present the man and the girl on a boundless plain standing by their dead ponies after a furious ride (a truly Crane touch.). I made some objections. A boundless plain in the light of a sunset could be got onto a backcloth, I admitted, but I doubted whether we could induce the management of any London theatre to deposit two stuffed horses on its stage.[32]

This stillborn play could nonetheless engender Conrad's "The Planter of Malata" thirteen years later. The action of that story has, as Conrad calls it, "the shadow of the primary idea" of *The Predecessor*, and "now and then, as I wrote, I had the feeling that he had the right to come and look over my shoulder." "Shadow" is an apt descriptive term, since the play was to have dealt with doubles—and the *doppelgänger* motif would, in the fiction, take center stage. "The Planter of Malata" is one of Conrad's most explicit and least resonant deployments of a fictive second self, and he concludes by mourning that:

> There will never be any collaboration for us now. But I wonder, were he alive whether he would be pleased with the tale. I don't know. Perhaps not. Or, perhaps, after picking up the volume with that detached air I remember so well, and turning over page after page in silence, he would suddenly read aloud a line or two and then looking straight into my eyes as was his wont on such

occasions, say with all the intense earnestness of affection that was in him: "I—like—that, Joseph."[33]

The Predecessor produced, arguably, a far more important result. Very soon after Crane's offer, and with what may well have been the sense of a chance earlier missed, Conrad proposed to Ford that they become collaborators. This association was longer, more fruitful and troubled than that of Conrad and Crane—but it had its taproot there. Crane and Ford were apposite in age and energy, if opposite in temperament. As Bernard Meyer convincingly shows in his *Joseph Conrad: A Psychoanalytic Biography*, the familyless Pole required a series of sibling surrogates to power his own artistic impulse. And if Ford was Conrad's "secret sharer," then his "predecessor" was Crane.

The support they gave each other was unstinting. Crane ballyhooed "The Nigger" to Hamlin Garland and others; he wrote of his "unancient mariner" with both warmth and pride. In a *Bookman* article, Crane announced: ". . . his novel is a marvel of fine descriptive writing. It is unquestionably the best story of the sea written by a man now alive, and as a matter of fact, one would have to make an extreme search among the tombs before he who has done better could be found . . ."[34] This was substantial praise indeed from the author of "The Open Boat," and Conrad reciprocated. He said in "A Note Without Dates" that Crane "had a wonderful power of vision which he applied to things of this earth and of our mortal humanity."[35] He struck this note often in public, though when writing directly to Crane, he sounded less austere. "I am envious of you—horribly. Confound you—you fill the blamed landscape—you—by all the devils—fill the seascape. The boat thing is immensely interesting. I don't use the word in its common sense. It is fundamentally interesting to me. Your temperament makes old things new and new things amazing . . ."[36] (Compare the recollection of Edith Ritchie Jones: "One day Mr. James and Stephen were having a discussion about something, and Stephen was getting the better of the argument. Suddenly Mr. James said, 'How old are you?' 'Twenty-seven,' said Stephen. 'Humph,' said Mr. James, 'prattling babe!' ")[37]

It is important to repeat that in the year 1900 both Conrad and James would have had to defer to the "prattling babe" in terms of public praise. They may have been his masters in craft—and acknowledged by him as such—but where Crane went and what he wrote was news. This must have made his elders restive if not downright envious; there is some chariness here. In a letter to Edward Garnett, Conrad expressed reservations:

> He has outline, he has colour, he has movement, with that he ought to go very far. But—will he? I sometimes think he won't. It is not an opinion—it is a feeling. I could not explain why he disappoints me—why my enthusiasm withers as soon as I close the book. While one reads, of course, he is not to be questioned. He is the master of his reader to the very last line—then—apparently for no reason at all—he seems to let go his hold. It is as if he had gripped you with greased fingers. His grip is strong but while you feel the pressure on your flesh you slip out from his hand—much to your own surprise. This is my stupid impression and I give it to you in confidence. It just occurs to me that it is perhaps my own self that is slippery. I don't know. You would know. No matter.[38]

The letters of Conrad confirm just this sense of the slippery self. Yet by comparison with his circumlocutions elsewhere, his approach to and dealings with Crane are direct. Some of the superlatives are forced, perhaps, and some of the supportiveness might seem to be routine—but the trust and amity ring true. One proof of this, and a substantial one, is that Conrad continued to write of his friend long after Crane's early death. He had nothing to gain then and no one to please, yet the introduction to the Beer biography is one of the final literary labors Conrad undertook. His previous essays, "Stephen Crane: A Note Without Dates" and "His War Book," helped to spark the revival, and there is pathos in his answer to an inquiring stranger—this in 1912: "Sad but true. I hardly meet anyone now who knows or remembers anything of him. For the younger oncoming writers he does not exist, simply. One or two have heard of the Red Badge and asked me 'what sort of thing it is. Is it worth looking at.' "[39]

The answer, for Conrad, was continually yes. He may have had some notion of vitality come full circle, or that it was time to try a summing-up—but he mourned Crane if anything more keenly as his own career wound down. The red sun at the end of *Lord Jim* may well have been derivative of Crane's "bloody wafer" in *The Red Badge of Courage*. Conrad's novel was composed more or less coeval with his friend's collapse, so Crane could have been a model for the young romantic. I do not mean to argue that *Lord Jim* is a *roman à clef*, with Stephen as its hero, but Conrad might well ponder "the destructive element" as it pertained to Brede. The image of Crane as a critical ghost who reads "The Planter of Malata" comes twenty-three years after Crane's death and one year before Conrad's own.

The families, too, remained friends. If James would applaud Cora's decision to return to America (and therefore her decision to leave his neighborhood), Conrad appeared to lament it. If Jessie Conrad never quite had veto power over Joseph's guests, her "Recollections of Stephen Crane" are warm. The two accepted an invitation to Ravensbrook immediately after their son's birth, and one of Conrad's sorrows was that Crane did not live long enough to teach Borys how to ride. He writes of Crane repeatedly as happiest on horseback, with a dog or two cavorting at his heels. The men shared a sailboat, *La Reine*, planning to moor it half the time at Folkestone and the other half at Rye. (Characteristically, Crane could not pay his part of the debt to Captain G.F.W. Hope—and Cora proposed, in 1900, that their half share of the boat be taken over by a wood merchant to whom they owed money. Whether he planned to sail or burn the thing is not clear, but Conrad paid off alone.)

When Conrad writes of their final meeting, it is in the accents of loss:

> I saw him for the last time on his last day in England. It was in Dover, in a big hotel, in a bedroom with a large window looking on the sea. He had been very ill and Mrs. Crane was taking him to some place in Germany, but one glance at that wasted face was enough to tell me that it was the most forlorn of all hopes. The last words he breathed out to me were: "I am tired. Give my love to your wife and child." When I stopped at the door for another look I saw that he had turned his head on the pillow and was staring wistfully out of the window at the sails of a cutter yacht that glided slowly across the frame, like a dim shadow against the grey sky.[40]

Wells was less solemn by nature, and less a pessimist. He had devised the game on the rush floor that would have been carpeted had Crane had the funds; he tried to tease his friend:

> As an expert in haemorrhages, I would be prepared to bet you any reasonable sum—I'll bet an even halo only I am afraid of putting you on that high mettle of yours—that haemorrhages aren't the way you will take out of this terrestial Tumult. . . . And confound it! what business have you in the Valley? It isn't midday yet and Your

Day's Work handsomely started I admit, is still only practically started. The sooner you come out of that Valley again and stop being absolutely irrelevant to your work, the better![41]

He would have lost the bet. In the language of "The Open Boat," the conclusion of Crane's life was "most wrongfully and barbarously abrupt." Wells's account of their final meeting—though written weeks and not decades after the event—is markedly similar to Conrad's:

I saw him for the last time hardly more than seven weeks ago. He was then in a hotel at Dover, lying still and comfortably wrapped about, before an open window and the calm and spacious sea. If you would figure him as I saw him, you must think of him as a face of a type very typically American, long and spare, with very straight hair and straight features and long, quiet hands and hollow eyes, moving slowly, smiling and speaking slowly, with that deliberate New Jersey manner he had, and lapsing from speech again into a quiet contemplation of his ancient enemy. For it was the sea that had taken his strength, the same sea that now shone, level waters beyond level waters, with here and there a minute, shining ship, warm and tranquil beneath the tranquil evening sky.[42]

The last work of his life was a new departure. It occupied Crane entirely during 1900, and it was—though after the fact and only by necessity—a collaboration. Its title, *The O'Ruddy*, came very near the end. Earlier, he had referred to it as *The Irish Romance* and even *Romance*; Cora so describes it in her letters to Pinker. (In this, as with *The Predecessor*, Crane anticipates Conrad's alliance with Ford. The latter pair spent six years intermittently at work on their *Romance*. As genre if not title, it seemed to authors of the time as sure a road to Easy Street as was the theater. They were wrong.)

That Brede Place would permit Crane to work was the theme of his letters from Brede. And *The O'Ruddy* seemed the path of least resistance. He had small stomach for or ability at research; Kate Lyon Frederic did most of the reading for Crane's other project of the period, *Great Battles of the World*. Her family name, O'Mahony, figured in Harold Frederic's own "Irish Romance," so Crane may also here have been saluting his dead friend. Frederic had introduced him to Ireland, and they had talked of an extended stay there together. Ireland would furnish a ready locale for good-humored antic plotting—and he wanted to incorporate his newfound knowledge of Brede.

He took few notes. He was feeling his way in this new form and tone, but doing so at speed. Crane's surviving plan for the novel reads in its entirety:

CHAPTER I

In which the reader is introduced to a very wise and adventuresome young man who seems almost certain to do great things before the end of the book.

CHAPTER II

Valiantly assisted by a friend, our hero fights a duel.

CHAPTER III

Our hero goes in search of a thief and meets only a highwayman.

CHAPTER IV

Finding the business of a gentleman rather arduous on an income of one guinea per the-rest-of-his-natural-life our hero turns highwayman and becomes interested.[43]

The figure of the bumbling brave *picaro*-cum-lover is not perhaps original, nor is the romantic interest all that interesting. Crane bit off more than he chewed. But the pervasive *brio* of the work is available even to the reader who does not know its dark personal concomitant; there are charm and exuberance throughout. Lines like these are representative: "But Paddy was an honest man even if he did not know it."[44] ". . . a lot of machinery so ingenious that it would require a great lack of knowledge to thoroughly understand it."[45] His synopsis can but suggest the entanglements of situation and the breezy narrative style.

Given Crane's habitual haste of composition, however, it is hard to see the plot as more than episodic and hard to predict how it would have been resolved. The notes he dictated to Cora while at Badenweiler provide no real instruction. This was a sticking point for those writers whom Cora approached at Crane's death. Their number and names, if not legion, are grim reminders of the program of *The Ghost*.

Robert Barr was Crane's deathbed choice to complete *The O'Ruddy*. He, too, had been at Dover and the Lord Warden Hotel. On June 8, 1900, he informed Karl Harriman:

> When your letter came I had just returned from Dover, where I stayed four days to see Crane off for the Black Forest. There was a thin thread of hope that he might recover, but to me he looked like a man already dead. When he spoke or rather whispered, there was all the accustomed humor in his sayings. I said to him that I would go over to the Schwarzwald in a few weeks, when he was getting better, and that we would take some convalescent rambles together. As his wife was listening he said faintly, "I'll look forward to that," but he smiled at me and winked slowly, as much as to say, "You damned humbug, you know I'll take no more rambles in this world."[46]

Barr appears to have agreed to work on *The O'Ruddy* more as a gesture than in expectation of fact; he did so in the spirit of their proposed "convalescent rambles together." The first real choice was Rudyard Kipling. Kipling declined the project sight unseen; his response makes the case for the artist as solitary. " 'My own opinion is & I hold it very strongly that a man's work is personal to him, & should remain as he made it or left it. I should have been glad to have done him a kindness, but this is not a thing that a man feeling as I do, can undertake.' "[47]

Cora was more than a typist for his finished drafts. She took dictation, emended, and rewrote. On April 7, 1900, in a revelatory request for quick money, she wrote Pinker: "Let me know if Serial is sold. If Mr. Crane should die, I have notes of end of novel so it could be finished & no one will lose—if that thought should occur."[48] She was not therefore blind to his disease or unaware of its gravity. After Kipling had had his say, she turned to H. B. Marriott-Watson. He took two days to read the manuscript and, with regrets, withdrew. Then A.E.W. Mason took the better part of two years before he pronounced himself unable to finish the book. By this time the theatrical entrepreneur, David Belasco, had given up on plans to turn the novel into a play—and there was protracted wrangling over who owed what to whom. Robert Barr did finally complete the romance, and *The O'Ruddy* appeared, with both names on the title page, in 1903.

Barr did little rewriting of the early chapters; Crane had planted what his collaborator later on dug up. But such characters as Forister and Colonel Royale disappear from the tale, while Father Donovan returns and a barrister is introduced. The finished text is nothing if not wellmade; Barr made O'Ruddy literate and had him pen his history surrounded by his loved ones in Brede Place. From Chapter Twenty-five on (the novel has thirty-three), the text is entirely Barr's; the ending is conventional and brief. In a letter to Willis Clarke, Barr says of his "predecessor," "Only a fourth of the book is really his, in the strict sense of the word 'his,' but I tried to carry through the spirit suggested for the whole."[49] Though his arithmetic exaggerates the case, his attempt to sustain the book's "spirit" is real. Yet spirit is wanting if willing; the smugglers, trapdoors, and yeomen of Brede are sketchy at best. And because Barr wanted to finish things off, the O'Ruddy demonstrates an unwonted efficiency in attaining his dear goal.

The book paid off some debts—those to Pinker in particular—but it did not do well. Where Crane had had control in the matter, collaboration had been functional; it cut corners or saved time. The system (with Cora or Kate Lyon Frederic) was an extension of his experience as journalist: four hands type faster than two. And the experience of theater is collaborative, or ought to be; few texts can be performed verbatim as composed. So what he cheerfully proposed for the stage (*The Predecessor, The Ghost*) comes to little indeed on the page. Among the several other shames of his death at twenty-eight, it is a shame he had no chance to test his mettle with an artist of the front rank. The conclusion was a final falling-off.

As the first first-person narrative in Crane's fiction, however, *The O'Ruddy* might have proved a vivid picaresque. Even truncate and rearranged, it represents an improvement over his conventional romance, *Active Service* (1899). And Crane's projected fictions could well have turned out as startling as were, in retrospect, *Maggie* and *The Red Badge of Courage*. The single constancy in that brief life had been consistent change. The transition he made in personal terms from Port Jervis to Brede was relatively smooth; it is possible the idiom of his art would equally have altered. He could not long have remained in the company of such self-conscious craftsmen without increasingly conscious application to the problems of craft. The alternative would have been hackwork. And he was too proud for that. Though he told Wells, "I got to" send sketches off to Pinker, he had a fitful integrity: the business of paying off his creditors was a separate account. According to Cora's notebook, when she suggested that he write for pure plain cash, "He turned on me & said: 'I will write for one man & banging his fist on writing table & that man shall be myself etc. etc.' "[50]

What then are we to make of this first figure in the group? He is not more enigmatic than Conrad or reticent than James, but his death at twenty-eight has enforced a kind of mystery. Crane never had the time to explain himself. Autobiography has of late become a young man's privilege, but the first-person confessional mode was alien to Crane. He had little inclination to be introspective, even at a time of life when self-scrutiny abounds. Henry Fleming, the most inward of his characters, is scarcely a self-portrait—and oratory was repugnant to him from the start.

The ethos of personal reticence is interestingly widespread in American authors. If the English keep their upper lips stiff, then the Americans keep them buttoned. . . . Consider, for example, the characters in Faulkner. He who talks well and fluently is almost always suspect, or at any rate too talkative. The inarticulate or quiet man will be by contrast gifted with the poetry of gesture. True eloquence resides in action, or beneath the level of conscious utterance. And think of Melville's heroic near-mutes: Queequeg, Bartleby, Billy Budd. Crane is of this company, a busy wordsmith busily debunking language. The colloquial usage is fine, the tall tale can be told at length —but the profession of "author" is one we should blush to confess.

On the other hand and given the nature of the beast, "confession" can well be invented. It sustains attention; it captures the listening ear. The novelist creates a host of

characters and must give them inner mass; as the lady in
E.M. Forster's adage puts it, "How can I know what I
think until I see what I say?" So garrulity, too, can mislead
or be counterfeit: the deep truth trotted out on the page
may prove an outright lie. Here the genres of fiction and
autobiography merge. We've all had the experience of forgotten history: the slightly tailored tale, the story told so
carefully we tell it letter perfect several times in the same
night. Or self-engendered history: an anecdote about our
childhood that we can't remember if we remember, or
remember having been told to remember. The novelist
imagines history. His protagonist has a maiden aunt, for
instance, and she has a birthday. We must be told where
the party takes place, whether she prefers chocolate or
carrot cake, if her rejected suitor still wears argyles after
his operation for cataracts that winter, and what the
weather is this afternoon of August 23 . . .

Crane's literary criticism is next to nonexistent and his
aesthetic unformed. He could, however, be a clear-eyed
reader when he chose. His opinion as to Wells's work
might have been heeded with profit: "I should say that
Mr. Wells will write better and better when he sticks to
characters altogether and does not so much concern himself with narrative. I may be wrong but it seems to me
that he has a genius for writing of underclass people
more honestly than Charles Dickens. . . ."[51] Wells said
that Crane had "no critical chatter," but he missed the
point. Part of the cowboy construct has to do with taci-
turnity; when Wells gossiped with an old school friend
during a poker game, Crane turned to them and said that,
in America, they'd be shot for such chitchat at cards.

Hamlin Garland and others have described him as
having a facility in composition that bordered on auto-
matic writing. Crane would enter a room and claim to
have a poem in his head, then sit and transcribe without

pause. The manuscripts document this; the image of artist as *vates* (possessed, hearing words in the wind of his skull) does not encourage revision.

Here we should consider Crane's youth. Lionized at twenty-five, he must have feared himself a cub; the heady admiration he received when come to England could only have gone to his head. He may have been self-conscious but not conscientiously so; one has the sense that he and Cora played "dress-up" in Brede Place. So there was an instinct for preservation, possibly, in "that deliberate New Jersey manner he had"—and irony would prove a saving grace. It is useful both in self-defense and for evaluating the flattery of others; it provides both an attitude to and distance from event. Most useful, perhaps, it organizes a response to experience before any such responsiveness can be entirely earned; with irony available, precocity counterfeits age.

Put it in comparative terms. At this point in their several careers, Crane, Ford, and Wells seemed similar indeed. They were facile to the point of fluency in prose and energetic to a fault; they were iconoclasts admitted to the Temple and invited to dine at the Club. They were each attracted to the attitude of upstart author as man of the world; they attitudinized a bit.

But Ford and Wells continued; their choices came clear over time. And it remains unclear, in the terms of this contrast, if Crane would have matured into an "old man mad about writing" or one who construed the novel to be useful if sufficiently instructive. He was, I believe, in a kind of equipoise for those final seasons at Brede—poised between his "Indians" and Conrad, or Madame Zipango's champagne and a discussion with the Master as to style. Put it another way: the choice of Brede Place was carefully made, and the neighborhood swarmed with artistic endeavor. But Stephen Crane in Havana was a different proposition. He traveled there from England and went incommunicado; there's more than a touch of comedy in Cora's long-distance attempts to haul her "husband" home. He had skipped out on his creditors before, and on women —but when he returned to Brede it was, fatally, to write. What he would have seen with his fine ironist's eye must be a matter of conjecture; "In the Country of Rhymers and Writers" is a fragment and unfinished.

To continue with comparatives: at twenty-eight Conrad had not even started to write, and the career of James was undistinguished. Crane's achievement is in part notable because he achieved so much and so quickly. *Maggie, The Red Badge of Courage,* and several of the enduring stories were behind him when he arrived. His first half year in England was productive, and excellently so; in addition to the journalism (war dispatches, "Irish Notes," "English Impressions") he produced such work as "The Monster," "Death and the Child," "The Bride Comes to Yellow Sky," and "The Blue Hotel." He was taken seriously as an author (far more so in England than America), and he met writers there that he took seriously. The library at Brede would furnish him examples of contemporary prose as well as of the classics. Crane appeared to read with close attention, as if once again at school. It was a very different company he sought from that of his companions in Greece or Cuba. His reverence was on the drift away from men of action and toward those men active in art.

Conrad represented both. It is for this reason, I think, that Crane so admired the Pole: Conrad described life as lived. (His prose of that period is no more directly autobiographical than was Crane's, but the data were authenticated by his very presence.) The fear of a "quick study" must surely be forgetfulness, that all is surface skill—and Crane might have feared that his own store of knowledge would be too quickly expended. By contrast, Conrad's sea lore would have seemed inexhaustible. Couple this with the manifest pains that the elder man took in piecing together his stories, and a role model stands forth intact: an artisan who knows whereof he writes. Conrad, "Jack ashore" yet at his work desk, would seem by 1900 to have attained that balance Crane sought: he had been to "darkest Africa" and was writing "Heart of Darkness"; he had sailed the Malay Archipelago and was composing *Lord Jim*.

In an early interview with an early mentor, "Howells Fears the Realists Must Wait," Crane quotes William Dean Howells as follows: "A writer of skill cannot be defeated because he remains true to his conscience. It is a long serious conflict sometimes, but he must win, if he does not falter. Lowell said to me one time: 'After all, the barriers are very thin. They are paper. If a man has his conscience and one or two friends who can help him it becomes very simple at last.' "[52]

Yet Crane's prose deteriorated with his health. One can argue whether or not "The Whilomville Stories" represent an advance over the "Sullivan County Sketches," but there can be no real doubt that the dying Crane failed to maintain the standard of his early work. This poses a real problem for the student of his writing, since the paradox is manifest: coeval with his seeming decision to apprentice himself to a craft, Crane's achievement tapered off. Critics have not put it precisely this way, but few have failed to tax him for his final frenzied prose. Received opinion has it that the move to Brede was murderous of the "natural" writer if not of the man entirely. Had he stayed at home or on the battlefield or not pretended to the English gentry or not written so much and for money—had he, in short, stayed the way that he was—then his "genius" too would have stayed. I have done less than justice to the argument, perhaps, but it misses an essential point: Crane was restless, and growth means change.

This quicksilver aspect of the man is reported on by all who knew him well. Some called it self-indulgence and some a self-destructive squandering of talent. Those with the advantage of hindsight were inclined to call it prophecy, as though Crane was sure he would die young. He told Nellie Crouse he did not care to live past thirty-five; he subtracted four years from that total for Karl Harriman, and the phrase in which he called himself "a dry twig on the edge of the bonfire" suggests the vision of his own impending end.

A continually interesting because unanswerable question of critical assessment is, in effect, *what if.* What if Crane had not gone to England, what if the doctor who misdiagnosed the gravity of his condition had been accurate, what if he had continued to follow Conrad and James's lead? The notion that Crane might have learned to take infinite pains in composition is far-fetched, but he was never predictable—and his proclaimed satisfaction with his final work is aimed much more at agents and publishers than at those who read him closely. The sad truth is that the tremendous output of his final year contains little of lasting value; his conceptions were feverish, and his attention wandered. But the *what if* remains; certain passages in *Wounds in the Rain, The O'Ruddy,* and the final stories are neither diminished nor spent. Had he recovered, so might have the prose.

The careers of American writers—in contrast, roughly, to those of Europeans—are the record of decline. There are exceptions to this rule, of course (a preeminent one is that of James), but the general pattern of early success entails a later failure. Cyril Connolly asserts, in *Enemies of*

Promise, that "the best that can happen for a writer is to be taken up very late or very early, when either old enough to take its measure, or so young that when dropped by society he has all life before him."[53] What would have happened to Crane had he "all life before him" is a riddle no reader can solve. His most famous book is not disguised autobiography or even personal experience; his work—unlike the conventional pattern established by the "one-book author"—proved various.

Crane was a wanderer and likely to have continued as such; when invalided, he talked of travel to the Transvaal or to Texas. One thing is certain, however; Port Jervis could not again represent home. He moved to England in part because of the rather more freewheeling mores as to marriage there; Harold Frederic, Wells, and Ford could live with women not their legal wives. With Cora as his mate, he would not be welcome back. The Crane family maneuvers against Cora after Stephen's death confirm the good sense of his decision to leave; it is no small irony that this ersatz cowboy and his quondam madam of a mistress hunted freedom in a manor house in Queen Victoria's land. "The Whilomville Stories" are in fact grounded in the landscape of his childhood, and they gain perspective from distance. As was the case with James, Crane wrote about America from England. He may have been briefly settling for the adulation of "Grub Street and Greenwich Village," the company of titled folk and the pretense at Brede—but he did not lose alertness. He took his subjects where he found them, turn by turn.

Yet, and this is crucial, he did so in his imaginative writing before the fact. His familiarity with the Bowery comes chronologically subsequent to *Maggie*; he had not seen a battle until *The Red Badge* established his credentials as a close witness of war. So the reportage and journalism should be read as ratification of previously invented worlds; the cart precedes the horse. He came to his auditions in the costume of the part, but it did look like acting a little . . .

Put in literary terms, this suggests he is far more a symbolist than realist—and his affinity with Conrad and James makes sense. Conrad wrote to Crane, "You are a complete impressionist," and elaborated this opinion in "A Note Without Dates," as well as when writing to Edward Garnett: "He is the only impressionist and only an impressionist."[54]

Wells thought the opposite. One of the first to salute Crane's work in England, Wells was also among the first to come forth with a memorial tribute. His "Stephen Crane From an English Standpoint" asserts affinity; he here describes an aesthetic, or rather a freedom therefrom, that makes Crane his brother-in-arms:

> In style, in method, and in all that is distinctively *not* found in his books, he is sharply defined, the expression in literary art of certain enormous repudiations. . . . Any richness of allusion, any melody or balance of phrase, the half-quotation that refracts and softens and enriches the statement, the momentary digression that opens like a window upon beautiful or distant things, are not merely absent, but obviously and sedulously avoided. It is as if the racial thought and tradition had been razed from his mind and its site plowed and salted. He is more than himself in this; he is the first expression of the opening mind of a new period, or at least, the early emphatic phase of a new initiative—beginning, as a growing mind must needs begin, with the record of impressions, a record of a vigor and intensity beyond all precedent.[55]

One can see here "the early emphatic phase" of what would be a more emphatic initiative still—and the expression that would go public with Wells's *Boon.* As early as 1900, and coincident with the century's start, Wells her-

alded "the opening mind of a new period." Yet what could
be more antithetical to the Impressionists than the obvious and sedulous avoidance of "any richness of allusion,
any melody or balance of phrase"? Wells means something very different by "the record of impressions" than
did Conrad, Ford, and James.

We tend as critics to ratify our own creative impulses.
The great theoreticians of language provide their readers
with a handbook as to how to read the great practitioners
—particularly if they be one and the same. We are given,
in effect, instruction on what to read how. Thus Pope, Coleridge, Arnold, Eliot, and the rest publish apologia under
the guise of analysis. Wells when praising Crane asserts
his own "enormous repudiations," whereas Ford would
make a map of Sussex with Crane at its center, standing
shoulder to shoulder with Conrad and James.

Crane himself avoided such assertion, and his death at
twenty-eight makes all enlistment moot. "In the Country
of Rhymers and Writers" is a satiric sketch, and his discussion of a proposed "American Academy" is etched in acid.
"I do not see why we should borrow this particular form
of laceration. It is never amusing; it only hurts. And it
accomplishes nothing."[56] In the end Crane proposes that
Edwin Markham, who photographs well, join the academy
alone. Nor, in his more serious "Concerning the English
Academy," does he fail to point out that the two main con-
tenders for the novelist's palm—James and Conrad—are
both foreigners. So it was not, and would not likely have
become, Crane's conclusion that a formal conclave of
writers has merit. There are soldiers and sailors who survive
because of fellowship—but the artist in "poor Steevie's"
work remains a solitary. The young man of sensibility may
be at the center of the canvas and by extension behind it
—but the self or group portrait here is merely a cartoon.

✿　　✿　　✿

Crane's death came quickly, six months into the century. This most American of authors had lived one third his writing life in England, and he died in Germany. So perhaps it was the sea that proved his "ancient enemy." Crane, in a review of *Under Two Flags*, wrote that Ouida "imitates the literary plan of the early peoples. They sang, it seems, of nobility of character."[57] In such a reading, surely, the Channel is Crane's Styx. After he had accumulated sufficient strength in Dover, they set out for the Continent. The trip to Badenweiler's sanatorium was doomed, and the processional they formed was that of a cortege. (Ford would experience similar establishments, though he would survive them.) Crane died on June 5, 1900.

The body was returned to lie in state in London, and on June 17 Cora sailed, with the casket, from Southampton. There was a service in New York, followed by interment in Hillside, New Jersey. Cora tried for a short time to manage in England alone; she could not. Brede Place was returned to the Frewens, and she returned to Jacksonville. The mark Crane left on his associates, and the memory preserved, was more personal than artistic. This is appropriate; he was a beginner at the end.

The following poem from Crane's *War Is Kind* may have been written with Conrad in mind. It is at any rate a testimonial to the power of shared sympathy; it stands as a fragment yet whole:

There was a man with tongue of wood
Who essayed to sing
And in truth it was lamentable
But there was one who heard
The clip-clapper of this tongue of wood
And knew what the man
Wished to sing
And with that the singer was content.[58]

III.
Conrad
and Ford

Once we were sitting in the front row of the stalls at the Empire. . . . And, during applause by the audience of some too middle-class joke, one of us leaned over towards the other and said, "Doesn't one feel lonely in this beastly country!" . . . Which of us it was that spoke neither remembered after, the other had been at that moment thinking so exactly the same thing.

—FORD MADOX FORD, *Joseph Conrad: A Personal Remembrance*, 1924

III.

Conrad and Ford

It was Conrad who made the suggestion. Collaboration was, for him, both a relief and release. He had urged it before and would do so again; his motives had been mixed. In *A Personal Record* he repeats a previous assertion: "What is it that Novalis says? 'It is certain my conviction gains infinitely the moment another soul will believe in it.' "[1] His years with Ford—of whom he asked the question and to whom he dictated the sentence— would test and confirm this belief.

As early as *Almayer's Folly*, Conrad had proposed a joint venture to his "aunt," Marguerite Poradowska. Before that book was accepted in England, he was requesting that she sponsor it in France. Eleven years his senior, Madame Poradowska was not a blood relation but a member of the literary establishment; some of his ambivalence toward such feminine sponsorship is captured in Marlow's reaction—described in "Heart of Darkness"—to the well-placed relative who gets him his command. Conrad's letters are those of a suitor, albeit at a distance and timid. If she accepted, he wrote, her name would grace the translation's title page, with his in small print and pseudonymously beneath. So the book is both a "proposal" and submission. His passion in this case would seem to have been a function of distance: he offered her his handiwork while holding back his hand.

Nothing came of the proposal, as nothing would come of the gambit with Crane. But the habit of unequal sharing was ingrained. Partnership for Conrad only rarely entailed parity; he would ride a seesaw with Ford. His father, Apollo, had been a poet and scholar who tutored Conrad in their exile—and the image of the dying Pole bent on translating Shakespeare must have remained value-charged. Conrad remembers his "first introduction to English literature" as a kind of command performance. The experience here re-created begins in secrecy and ends in alliance with Apollo; it is noteworthy, too, that Conrad pretends to grammatical confusion while playing on the title of the play:

My first acquaintance was (or were) the "Two Gentlemen of Verona," and that in the very MS. of my father's translation. It was during our exile in Russia, and it must have been less than a year after my mother's death, because I remember myself in the black blouse with a white border of my heavy mourning. We were living together, quite alone, in a small house on the outskirts of the town of T——. That afternoon, instead of going out to play in the large yard which we shared with our landlord, I had lingered in the room in which my father generally wrote. What emboldened me to clamber into his chair I am sure I don't know, but a couple of hours afterwards he discovered me kneeling in it with my elbows on the table and my head held in both hands over the MS. of loose pages. I was greatly confused, expecting to get into trouble. He stood in the doorway, looking at me with some surprise, but the only thing he said after a moment of silence was:

"Read the page aloud."[2]

The very act of translation is collaborative, a contract between practitioners with no reference to space or time. Surely Conrad's career in English literature has something to do with this seminal moment—the boy who clambers into his father's chair and finds himself praised, not punished. That he was told to "read aloud" is instructive also, as if language should be sonorous and heard. André Gide had Conrad as his more than silent partner when he undertook to publish the latter's work in France; Conrad suggested joint ventures to both Edward Noble and Richard Curle. (These came after the experience with Ford and would have been less wide-ranging. But it does seem a continual impulse in Conrad to want another person in the room.) He, like James and Crane, attempted to write for the theater; he even took a turn at presenting *Nostromo* in French.

Although his choice of partners may have seemed surprising, that Conrad hunted colleagues is less of a surprise. He was acutely alone; his marriage to Jessie George had exacerbated and not dispelled this sense of artistic isolation. He had begun a new *métier* and in a foreign tongue. Ford, too, was of European extraction; they both were recent fathers and in flight from domestic constraint. In James's usage of the term, if not that of actual coupling, their association has the feel of an "affair."

Ford begins his "personal remembrance" with this portrait:

He was small rather than large in height; very broad in the shoulder and long in the arm; dark in complexion with black hair and a clipped black beard. He had the gestures of a Frenchman who shrugs his shoulders frequently. When you had really secured his attention he would insert a monocle into his right eye and scrutinise your face from very near as a watchmaker looks into the works of a watch. He entered a room with his head held high, rather stiffly and with a haughty manner, moving his head once semicircularly. In this one movement he had expressed to himself the room and its contents; his haughtiness was due to his determination to master that room, not to dominate its occupants, his chief passion being the realisation of aspects to himself.[3]

Born in 1872 and younger even than Crane, Ford was long, lean, phlegmatic—Conrad's seeming opposite. At the time of their first meeting, he was a "small producer," making vegetable gardens and books. As he puts it:

In those days the writer had been overcome by one of those fits of agricultural enthusiasm that have overwhelmed him every few years, so that such descriptive writers as have attended to him have given you his picture in a startling alternation as a Piccadilly dude in top hat, morning coat and spats, and as an extremely dirty agricultural labourer.[4]

Wells asserts that the two "remain together, contrasted and inseparable in my memory." He and Ford had fallen out by the time he wrote the following, but it confirms the above:

What he is really or if he is really, nobody knows now and he least of all; he has become a great system of assumed *personas* and dramatized selves. His brain is an exceptionally good one and when first he came along, he had cast himself for the role of a very gifted scion of the Pre-Raphaelite stem, given over to artistic purposes and a little undecided between music, poetry, criticism, The Novel, Thoreau-istic horticulture and the simple appreciation of life.[5]

How this welter of identities would have resolved itself had Conrad not appeared is uncertain. Although Ford liked to think that Crane mistook him for a bailiff, in this instance he reports that Conrad, coming around the corner of the house, mistook him for the gardener. Certainly, however, Ford defined himself as author by the time of their collaboration's end. *Joseph Conrad: A Personal Remembrance* derives its title at least in part from Conrad's own *A Personal Record*. How much of Ford derives from Conrad, and how much of Conrad's artistry emerged because of Ford, is the subject of this chapter. Their intimacy spans the years from 1898 to 1909, and their friendship—though disrupted and impaired—survived at Conrad's death. Writing to Wells in 1905, Conrad proved more accurate than he could foresee: "Ford . . . is a sort of life-long habit—of which I am not ashamed, because he is a much better fellow than the world gives him credit for."[6]

The specifics of their association have been authoritatively documented.[7] What the data signify, however, remains open to interpretation. Conrad's changeability-cum-reticence and Ford's inventiveness have done much to confuse the issue, as have their partisans. Jessie Conrad was furious with Ford when his book appeared, and she shredded it whole cloth. Her own recollections (*Joseph Conrad As I Knew Him*, and *Joseph Conrad and His Circle*) routinely damn the interloper—or damn him with faint praise. Any account of so long a partnership must perforce be partial. Nor are we likely to resolve a problem of process; it is not a question of innocence and guilt, or major and minor allocations of responsibility. We do not need to read the work as if before competing claimants— as though the scholar were Solomon and *Romance* a disputed child.

Take the following example. Conrad's first experience of

England came from a steamer that docked at Lowestoft, and Ford used to vacation nearby. On various occasions, according to Ford:

> Conrad could bring himself to remember there a little boy with long golden hair, a bucket and a spade, who used to march up to the young able seaman and ask him questions in an unintelligible tongue . . . And indeed, in moments of *great* effusiveness, patting the writer on the shoulder, Conrad used to assert that it was one of the writer's books, seen on the bookstall of Geneva railway station, that had first turned his thoughts to writing English as a possibility.[8]

There are several fictions here. Conrad was seventeen years Ford's senior, so it is within the limits of chronological possibility that they met on the beach at Lowestoft—but the likelihood is slim. The beach in any case would have had a number of blond boys with buckets and spades. It is even less likely that Ford's juvenilia occasioned Conrad's first thoughts of writing in English. Taken out of context, this is the sort of braggadocio that sets critical teeth on edge; it's more appropriate to point to Shakespeare and Apollo.

Yet the context establishes indirect discourse—he ascribes the invention to Conrad—and Ford's own disbelief. " 'So it couldn't be me,' as the old mare said. But nothing would have pleased Conrad's generous and effusive moods better than to claim the writer as his literary godfather. He was like that."[9]

The question therefore modulates from fact or fancy to whose fantasy do we read here? Bernard Meyer cites this passage as an instance of Conrad's deep kinship with Ford, and of his desire to consolidate their linkage. As invented history and an imagined episode, it partakes of the "Family Romance"; the father figure claims the son as his own "literary godfather." But Ford would not have reported on such "generous and effusive moods" had the idea not struck him; from his present vantage in 1924, it ratifies—if only via his denial—their mythopoeic shared past. Conrad landed at Lowestoft in 1878 and met Ford twenty years later; by 1924 Ford, too, would telescope time. So even if the connection is false, its very iteration imposes a connective—and the wishful feel of the passage attaches to both authors equally.

They met via Edward Garnett. Ford had done some research on the trial of Aaron Smith, the last man tried for piracy in the British courts. Aaron Smith had been acquitted, and the accounts of his adventures occasioned what would become *Romance*. Ford apparently regaled his guests with anecdotes about the case; Garnett may have brought Conrad along on purpose, with some such entertainment in mind. Crane was in Cuba and Conrad still stalled on *The Rescue*; *The Daily Mail's* review of his *Tales of Unrest* had pointed to his slipshod grammar and "laxities of style." Ford, on the other hand, was nothing if not fluent; at twenty-four he had already published a novel, *The Shifting of the Fire*, a volume of poems, several volumes of fairy tales, and a biography of his maternal grandfather, Ford Madox Brown.

Conrad made inquiries, and then he made his approach. It is difficult to disentangle motive now, or to evaluate the various assertions. The question is a vexed one, and most answers are polemical. They range from the theory that Conrad could and would have written nothing of value without the inspiriting presence of Ford to the claim that Ford was "a fat patronizing slug upon the Conradian lettuce."[10] Henry James, according to Garnett, thought the project doomed. "To me this is like a bad dream which one relates at breakfast! Their traditions and their gifts are so dissimilar. Collaboration between them is to me inconceivable."[11] Wells, too, disapproved. He bicycled over to Aldington to warn Ford off; much to the latter's chagrin, "he said that I should probably ruin Conrad's 'delicate Oriental style.' "[12] In retrospect, however, Wells conceded that Ford was of use. "I think Conrad owed a very great deal to their early association; Hueffer helped greatly to 'English' him and his idiom, threw remarkable lights on the English literary world for him . . . and conversed interminably with him about the precise word and about perfection in writing."[13]

Beyond cavil this "welded collaboration" was the idea of the elder man. As the partnership took shape, Conrad explained himself to W. H. Henley:

> When talking with Hueffer my first thought was that the man there who couldn't find a publisher had some good stuff to use and that if we worked it up together my name, probably, would get a publisher for it. On the other hand I thought that working with him would keep under the particular devil that spoils my work for me as quick as I turn it out (that's why I work so slow and break my word to publishers), and that the material being of the kind that appeals to my imagination and the man being an honest workman we could turn out something tolerable—perhaps; and if not he would be no worse off than before. It struck me the expression he cared for was in verse; he had the faculty; I have not; I reasoned that partnership in prose would not affect any chances he may have to attain distinction—of the real kind—in verse. It seemed to me that a man capable of the higher form could not very much care for the lower. These considerations encouraged me in my idea.[14]

Ford seems to have given it less careful thought; he jumped at the suggestion. It is to his reportage after the fact, however, that we owe most of what we know about the collaboration. And since his memoirs are at least in part fiction, we should disengage the several strands with care. What follows are impressions of Impressionists; my opinions are offered as such.

First, and in contrast to Conrad, Ford was habitually generous. He loaned Conrad money as well as his house; as late as 1927 he would offer his roof to the Borys Conrad family. It was his book, after all, that the two were proposing to share, his research and preliminary pages of which they made use. The event did prove Conrad correct; *Romance* would "get a publisher" because of his efforts and name. Yet the pattern once established would remain: in each of the three instances of their coauthored texts, the plot was provided by Ford. He would make light of this, dismissing "subject matter" as immaterial; still, it is a *sine qua non*.

Ford's grandfather had taught him to "beggar yourself rather than refuse assistance to any one whose genius you think shows promise of being greater than your own."[15] This was a lesson Ford learned. He may have been self-aggrandizing but rarely at the expense of others; his career was predicated on the notion that a writer helps writers who ask for the help. To be sure, he construed such requests rather widely and his offer of aid would sometimes seem like meddling—but the characteristic note of the collaboration is that Conrad required assistance.

It bears repeating that Ford, like Crane, had a precocious facility in composition; the writing of a book was no major challenge or feat. Instead, and as Wells suggests, Ford wanted to be thought a dilettante. The term was not pejorative; it conveyed the offhand competency of a gentleman's attainments. "In the Middle Ages they used to say that the proper man was one who had written a book, built a house, planted a tree and begotten a child."[16]

To one who espoused this credo, the continual close scrutiny of language must have come as a surprise. It was all very well to write poetry and to have proficiency in Provençal, but a novel was not something one toiled at long or hard. Ford had taken art for granted till he took Conrad on. Collaboration may have been intended to expedite matters, but it had the opposite effect: the work that is their most thoroughly shared venture (*Romance*) took the longest to complete. Conrad was never casual; he calculated both cause and probable effect. He needed Ford's sheer energy and verve. The "particular devil" of which he writes to Henley—uncertainty—did not torment his partner. And Ford at twenty-four was willing willy-nilly; he must have been flattered by the proposal and susceptible to change. One of his less defensible statements (though technically correct in terms of the quantity of publication) is that he was the better known and "boomed" author of the two; the reverse is the truth. They each had something to gain. But neither of them could have known how large a gain would ensue.

In *Return to Yesterday*, Ford summarizes it thus:

> Literary collaborations seem to present to the public aspects of mystery which they do not deserve. They are rare. It is unusual for two persons of inter-supportable temperaments to come together and bear each other's society, day in day out, for the long space of time that it takes to write a book. Few books can be written in a very short time; collaboration slows down writing, if only for material reasons. *Romance* by Conrad and myself was more than five years in the writing. Whether the book itself was worth the labour, it is for the public rather than myself to say. But that the labour in itself was worth while for us I have no doubt at all. I, at least, learned the greater part of what I know of the technical side of writing during the process, and Conrad certainly wrote with greater ease after the book had been in progress some while.[17]

* * *

Shortly before "the process" began, the Conrads leased Pent Farm. The writers' early commerce had more to do with the business of moving than novels, since Ford owned the place. (He would claim that he relinquished this charmed haven in Conrad's honor. But the fact is that Ford's wife, Elsie, had conceived a dislike for the isolation of Pent Farm, and they had moved out earlier. The interim tenant was the painter Walter Crane.)

Pent Farm is located at Postling near Hythe, and Conrad would remain there until 1907. This substantial cottage, with its steep-sloped roofs and wooden porch above the door, hosted a substantial cottage industry; Conrad rarely left it and rarely left off working. Chockablock with relics from the Pre-Raphaelite movement, it gave him great pleasure; he liked to think that he was working at Christina Rossetti's table, by the light of a Morris lamp. If there be a genius of place, Pent Farm may lay claim to it. On arrival, Conrad composed "Heart of Darkness," and his major period is coincident with his tenancy. One reason for the move was precisely its location; Conrad felt at the center of things.

The Pent contrives to be both central and aloof; it sits in a small hollow in the bend of a small lane. It proved far more a haven than did the mansion at Brede, and it may rival Lamb House as a locus for achievement. On December 18, 1898, when settled at his new address, Conrad wrote Aniela Zagorska:

It is better here . . . Before my window I can see the buildings of the farm, and on leaning out and looking to the right, I see the valley of the Stour, the source of which is so to speak behind the third hedge from the farmyard. Behind the house are the hills (Kentish Downs) which slope in zigzag fashion down to the sea,

like the battlements of a big fortress. A road runs along
the foot of the hills near the house—a very lonely and
straight road, and along which (so it is whispered) old
Lord Roxby—he died 80 years ago—rides sometimes at
night in a four-in-hand driven by himself. . . . We live
like a family of anchorites. From time to time a pious pil-
grim belonging to la grande fraternité des lettres comes
to pay a visit to the celebrated Joseph Conrad—and to
obtain his blessing. Sometimes he gets it and sometimes
he does not, for the hermit is severe and dyspeptic et
n'entend pas la plaisanterie en matière d'Art![18]

That December night Conrad hosted Galsworthy. To
illustrate the effect of his residence in Pent Farm, however, let us trace Conrad's friendship with Wells. At first,
and as in the first meeting with Crane, the encounter took
place on professional grounds. (Wells had reviewed
Conrad favorably in *The Saturday Review*; according to
the former, "it was his first 'important' recognition and he
became anxious to make my acquaintance."[19]) On May
25, 1896, Conrad's letter thanking Wells has something of
a politic gratitude:

Dear Sir,

If I prized highly the review before I knew who wrote
it—it becomes still more precious now, when the name of
my kind appreciator is known . . .[20]

Just before the move from Stanford-le-Hope, on October 11, 1898, Conrad could cite anticipated proximity as a
reason:

My dear Mr. Wells,

I am writing in a state of jubilation at the thought we
are going to be nearer neighbors than I dared to hope a
fortnight ago. We are coming to live in Pent Farm which
is only a mile or so from Sandling Junction . . .[21]

By November 17 both the salutation and the tone had changed:

My dear Wells,

I was glad to find you well enough to be out for an airing, though of course horribly sorry to miss you. I couldn't wait. A man was coming to see me whom I had to meet at Sandling. I only made a dash to Sandgate to hear how you were getting on . . .[22]

As of 1900 Wells would be "My dear H.G.," and there is an undated letter shortly thereafter that begins, "Dearest H. G. . . ." Conrad has traveled a considerable distance from the original "Dear Sir." This undated letter bemoans the slight remaining distance: "Seriously I much rather talk with you than write, as in the last case one tries to be brief . . ."[23] The letters of the group have been in part preserved; their conversations have of course been lost. We profit, paradoxically, from each meeting missed.

With the exception of those authors who undertake a formal career partnership, I know of no arrangement more productive than Conrad and Ford's. To list the documented collaboration is to establish its extensiveness. The collaboration began almost at once, on the pirate's story then titled *Seraphina.* Aaron Smith was called John Kemp (a name incised on one of the windows of Pent Farm), and *Seraphina, Romance.* The two are jointly listed as the authors of *The Inheritors, Romance,* and "The Nature of a Crime." Ford may have had a hand in *Chance, The Rescue,* "Gaspar Ruiz," and "Heart of Darkness"; he most certainly did in *Nostromo.* He provided at least the idea for "Amy Foster" and *The Secret Agent*—the latter attested by Conrad, the former asserted by Ford.

Equally important was Ford's role as scribe. It entailed more than transcription. The model of simultaneous translation seems applicable, as if Conrad's spoken tongue required alteration for the page. On those occasions when Conrad "wrote" quickly, Ford employed shorthand; he took dictation. Often he drew Conrad out, urging his recalcitrant and gout-ridden partner to produce:

> I would manoeuvre him towards writing as the drake manoeuvres the sitting duck back to the nest when she has abandoned her eggs. I would read over his last sentence to him. If it provoked no beginnings on his part I would displace him at the desk and write a sentence or two.[24]

He copied out the dialogue for Conrad's play *One Day More*, and helped with restoring the burned pages of "The End of the Tether." In this instance, and in order to meet a publisher's deadline, Conrad moved to Winchelsea. There they worked—according to both Mrs. Conrad and Ford—late nights every night:

> It became a matter of days; then of hours. Conrad wrote; the writer corrected the manuscript behind him or wrote in a sentence—the writer in his study on the street, Conrad in a two-roomed cottage that we had hired immediately opposite. The household sat up all night keeping soups warm.[25]

Ford was instrumental—indispensable, even—in Conrad's books *The Mirror of the Sea* and *A Personal Record*. First published in England as *Some Reminiscences*, they have the feel of conversation, its rhetoric and form. As Conrad handsomely admitted in 1923, Ford was much more than a sounding board: "The mere fact that it was the occasion of your putting on me that gentle but persistent pressure which extracted from the depths of my then despondency the stuff of the *Personal Record* would be enough to make its memory dear."[26]

Ford's description of this process bears reproducing at length:

> *The Mirror of the Sea* and *A Personal Record* were mostly written by my hand from Conrad's dictation. Whilst he was dictating them, I would recall incidents to him—I mean incidents of his past life which he had told me but which did not come freely back to his mind because at the time he was mentally ill, in desperate need of money and, above all, skeptical as to the merits of the reminiscential form which I had suggested to him. The fact is I could make Conrad write at periods when his despair and fatigue were such that in no other way would it have been possible to him. He would be lying on the sofa or pacing the room, railing at life and literature as practised in England, and I would get a writing pad and pencil and, whilst he was still raving, would interject: "Now, then, what was it you were saying about coming up the Channel and nearly running over a fishing boat that suddenly appeared under your bows?" and gradually there would come *Landfalls and Departures*. Or I would say: "What was the story you told of the spy coming with a sledgeful of British gold to your uncle's house in Poland in order to foment insurrection against Russia?" And equally gradually there would come the beginnings of *A Personal Record*. There are no episodes of my past life more vivid to me—you must remember that I had a great enthusiasm for my collaborator—than those dictations that mostly took place on a little terrace of my cottage at Aldington, high up in the air, with the great skies over the Romney Marsh below.[27]

The image of a "mentally ill" Conrad "railing at life and literature as practised in England" and "raving" until Ford could capture his attention is not one that pleases Conradians or that they can readily forgive Ford. But no one has disproved it, and the enduring legacy of the collaboration may well be these two books. It is, so far as I know, a special and surprising case—not Boswell recording a Johnson nor yet in the category of ghostwriting. Rather, and insofar as the autobiography is "as told to" Ford, it seems to have required his "gentle but persistent pressure" for the telling. The volumes are scarcely confessional, but no other stimulus caused Conrad to respond at length in "the reminiscential form." They are monologues, with the dialogue excised. It makes small difference if Conrad explained himself to his actual interlocutor alone, or if he had in mind an audience larger than one, since Ford provided both. He published what they produced.

The first installment of these memoirs appeared in the first issue of *The English Review*. (That issue, published in December 1908, also included "The Jolly Corner" by James, "A Fisher of Men" by Galsworthy, a W. H. Hudson essay on Stonehenge, an installment of Well's *Tono-Bungay*, and a Constance Garnett translation of Tolstoy!) Though Ford's claims to have begun the magazine in order to furnish Conrad with a forum are no doubt hyperbolic—others would say the same of a poem by Thomas Hardy—Conrad's reminiscences ran *seriatim* there. One occasion for their cooling-off came when Ford announced in print that Conrad was too ill to provide an eighth installment; Conrad insisted the book was complete. So we may call Ford a publisher and secretary as well as a coprogenitor; on the grounds of these two texts alone, he performed a service.

Nor are these the sole grounds. There are three further categories of collaboration. They are not discrete but contiguous; for the purposes of discussion, however, I shall separate them out. The three additional modes of partnership are represented here by "Amy Foster," *Nostromo*, and *Romance*.

Amy Foster was the name of Conrad's cook. So Jessie Conrad says, and she says further that the story of that name is Conrad's entirely. Ford Madox Hueffer may have walked with her husband by the seashore or near graveyards, she admits, but the genesis of "Amy Foster" had nothing to do with him. She is wrong.

In a letter to William Blackwood on November 7, 1900, Conrad demonstrates familiarity with Ford's just published *The Cinque Ports*. He acknowledges receipt of the book, then says:

> Hueffer's talent has been from the first sympathetic to me. Throughout, his feeling is true and its expression genuine with ease and moderation. He does not stand on his head for the purpose of getting a new and striking view of his subject. Such a method of procedure may be in favour nowadays but I prefer the old way, with the feet on the ground . . .[28]

The Cinque Ports is characteristically Fordian, even if the character was just being formed. No mean feat of scholarship, the book has charm as well as range. It remains a first-rate introduction to the region and should be republished today.

Conrad wrote to Blackwood, "There is—it seems to me —a good deal of force in his quiet phrasing. His facts I believe to be right. . . ." In *Return to Yesterday* and with reference to "Amy Foster," Ford claims that "I suggested the subject . . . in my *Cinque Ports* of 1902."[29] By 1931 he had gotten the date of publication wrong. But the assertion is right, as Conrad had said were his facts:

> One of the most tragic stories that I remember to have heard was connected with a man who escaped the tender mercies of the ocean to undergo an almost more merciless buffeting ashore. He was one of the crew of a German merchant that was wrecked almost at the foot of the lighthouse. A moderate swimmer, he was carried by

the current to some distance from the scene of the catastrophe. Here he touched the ground. He had nothing, no
clothes, no food; he came ashore on a winter's night. In
the morning he found himself in the Marsh near Romney.
He knocked at doors, tried to make himself understood.
The Marsh people thought him either a lunatic or a
supernatural visitor. To lonely women in the Marsh cottages he seemed a fearful object. . . . They warned their
menfolk of him, and whenever he was seen he was
hounded away and ill-used. He got the name of Mad
Jack.[30]

Whether Ford spoke the story aloud or Conrad read it
in the text is immaterial. There can be no doubt that this
is the story Conrad transformed, making of it "Amy
Foster." The key word here, however, is transformed—
and the process of such transformation is the process of
narrative art. The anecdote reproduced above has force
and pathos, certainly, but in this respect Jessie Conrad is
right: "Amy Foster" is far more her husband's accomplishment than Ford's. The tale of Yanko Gooral from the Car-
pathians, and his cruel treatment at the hands of English
provincials, is one of the most personal that Conrad ever
wrote. It can be read as a disguised psychobiography with
reference to his sense of displacement when their son,
Borys, was born; it can be read as a kind of expiation for
and reference to his previous sea change and flight from
landlocked Poland. It has been read as a self-reflexive
plaint about the limits of language and a tongue-tied
yearning after song; it may be read as an allegory with the
figure of Yanko as Christ. It has even been read as a parable of failed salvation, a description of exogamy, as evidence of Conrad's incipient nervous collapse and his
deep-rooted pessimism regarding the limits of love; it can
of course be read as all of these collectively. But such and
additional readings emerge from the story Conrad pub-

lished in December 1901, and not from the tale Ford tells.

His assertion, in 1924, that "Amy Foster (is) a short story originally by the writer which Conrad took over and entirely rewrote"[31] is almost surely false. It modulates, in *Return to Yesterday*, to a claim for the original impetus, not a draft. Ford may have withdrawn the larger claim in favor of the lesser and defensible one, or he may not have been conscious of disparity. But this is the sort of Solomon-like dissection of the body of a text that I earlier suggested is tangential to the real and lively case: Ford and Conrad were together daily, and "Amy Foster" is one of the several results.

The dynamic described above is collaboration at its outer extent and in the broadest definition of the word. It is the kind of process with which all writers are familiar —the gleaning of rags and twigs and mud with which we line our nests. Henry James in his Prefaces refers to such accretion continually, and how a story told in passing will stick with its listener until told again. For Ford, at any rate, "treatment" is the consequential thing; to give someone a topic is not to give him much. Though life be a series of irritants, not every grain of sand becomes a pearl. The "making" is all; Oedipus and Lear were histories to start with, and *Moby Dick* no more than a sailor's tall tale.

Take another example from *The Cinque Ports*. The following evokes the famous passage in "Heart of Darkness" wherein Marlow compares the mouth of the Thames to that of the Congo:

> One may think of those Northerners from their land of cold gray skies and beetling bird-crags sailing up the strange silent streams between the mournful flats and the little huts at the river's mouth. They went past the open ground, up the sluggish stream between the thick walls of tree-trunks. They saw strange folk flitting from trunk to trunk in the dark silence, heard strange cries echo

down the waveways. The boats panted up-stream. They were going into a strange land, a land of strange creeds, strange habits, unmeaning language, strange sacrifices. They went up-stream in that morning of the world, up-stream, holding their lives in their hands, as today our ships pant up unknown streams of an Africa not so remote, not so strange: as ships will pant up unknown streams until the end of time.[32]

This is more Conrad's subject than Ford's. His sense of the ongoing mystery of exploration informs "Heart of Darkness" throughout. Here is a single and similar instance:

> . . . the lower reaches of the Thames . . . had known the ships and the men. They had sailed from Deptford, from Greenwich, from Erith—the adventurers and the settlers; kings' ships and the ships of men on 'Change; captains, admirals, the dark "interlopers" of the Eastern trade, and the commissioned "generals" of East India fleets. Hunters for gold or pursuers of fame, they all had gone out on that stream, bearing the sword, and often the torch, messengers of the might within the land, bearers of a spark from the sacred fire. . . .
>
> "And this also," said Marlow suddenly, "has been one of the dark places on the earth."[33]

And here Ford writes of Brede Place in a fashion that prefigures both the smuggler's house in *Romance* and the mansion of *The O'Ruddy*. He says that "it has been long more or less abandoned—though it is at present inhabited" (by Stephen Crane) and tells the legend of "Giant Oxenbridge." He continues:

> Brede Place has altogether an uncanny local reputation; for one thing, the ground beneath it is riddled with underground passages running for miles and miles—who knows where? Lights, too, which cannot be humanly accounted for, have been seen glowing in the chapel win-

dows. As a matter of fact, it was once the headquarters of a band of smugglers who, not wishing to be troubled after nightfall, both spread reports to the discredit of the place and took steps to make bogies manifest to any bold spirit who ventured to disturb them at their trade. But the house is a noble house . . .[34]

These cases are similar to though not the equivalent of "Amy Foster." They illustrate a generalized awareness as well as particular parallel usage, a sharing of subjects that hang in the air. Ford claims (in a deleted passage from *A Personal Remembrance*, and later in an article, "Conrad and the Sea") to have paid "minute and letter-by-letter consideration" to the closing section of "Heart of Darkness." The two were together while Conrad corrected the proofs, and Ford's close analysis of the final paragraph does indeed pay "letter-by letter consideration" to the text at hand.

But whether he heard of the Brede Place smugglers before Crane and Robert Barr; whether he first described "the strange folk flitting from trunk to trunk in the dark silence" or emulated Conrad's description is trivial: the differences of usage are as striking as the similarities. If writers form a community, such communality of interest ought to be the rule. Congruence, or repetition—or even a kind of plagiarism—is not in such contexts a risk. Imitation is flattery's form. We do not fault a painter for lack of originality because he executes a Pietà or a crucifixion scene. Twenty novels about warfare do not eradicate the possibility of a splendid twenty-first. No two treatments of a theme will read alike; twenty sonnets "to his mistress' eyebrow" will be as various as the twenty sonneteers. We have a finite number of topics, and they may as well be shared.

Nostromo is a different proposition. Arguably, it evolves

from *Romance* in somewhat the manner that "Amy Foster" grows from the paragraph in *The Cinque Ports*. But Conrad had the notion, according to his preface, long before he worked with Ford—and the principal sources of the novel are located elsewhere. The Republic of Costaguana has its histories and previous texts, just as the figure of Nostromo has its model in Dominic Cervoni. Conrad's experience of South America was slight, his stay in Cartagena brief, and he perforce depended on research.

But few would wish to argue that *Nostromo* is derivative. It is a mirror held to nature, not to nature's mirror. Imagination ranges freely in it, and inventiveness abounds. The generally accepted masterpiece of Conrad's master period, it is both bigger and better than "Amy Foster." No other canvas in the *oeuvre* is so detailed yet complete; the artist's "signature" is unmistakable and evidenced on every page.

Ford wrote a chapter, however. He contributed at least fifteen manuscript pages to the installment that appeared in *T. P.'s Weekly*, April 8, 1904. This corresponds to a large portion of Chapter V, Part II ("The Isabels"), and the odds are he wrote rather more. Collaboration here was a matter of functional necessity; he describes it, many years later, to George T. Keating:

> The circumstances in which I wrote that small portion of *Nostromo* were as follows and are very simple and explicable. Whilst I was living in London with Conrad almost next door and coming in practically every day for meals, he was taken with so violent an attack of gout and nervous depression that he was quite unable to continue his installments of *Nostromo* that was then running as a serial in T.P.'s weekly. I therefore simply wrote enough from time to time to keep the presses going—a job that presented no great difficulties to me.[35]

Mr. Keating, the Conrad collector, had elicited this

explanation of the holograph pages in Ford's hand. Ford then protests too much: "I was practically under oath to Conrad not to reveal these facts owing to the misconceptions that might arise and nothing in the world would have induced me to reveal it now but for the extremely unfortunate sale of these pages." He made the same claim in public and was disbelieved. It may seem a teapot tempest, but the suggestion that Ford could so successfully ape Conrad's style as to escape detection aroused a storm of protest. His disclaimer did not help:

> ... Conrad could not have been ashamed of the fact that I wrote passages into his work and, I may presume that he would not now resent my mention of the fact. But, indeed, the importance of the passages I did write was negligible, and they themselves were so frequently emended out of sight that they could not make as much difference to the completion and glory of his prose as three drops of water poured into a butt of Malmsey.[36]

As J. H. Morey has shown, the manuscript in the Keating Collection proves Ford correct; if anything, he is too modest here. The passage was only slightly emended; Conrad felt no need to transform it "out of sight." It is written in haste and is—to my mind—a successful moment in the book. The interview between Antonia Avellanos and Martin Decoud has more of the feel of flesh-and-blood commerce between lovers than do the affairs of the Capataz de Cargardores, Nostromo himself. Their courtship in the drawing room is handled with authority. Such ease of utterance as " 'Martin, you will make me cry,' " is elsewhere denied the marmoreal Antonia. This sort of romantic encounter was not Conrad's *métier*.

I would even argue that Martin Decoud acquires dimension in the passage: the trifling *boulevardier* becomes a patriot and hero because of his love. That pas-

sion grows credible here. Ford said that he composed the
interview as a holding action—in order not to shift the
plot or introduce new characters. This permits him to
focus on the lovers, and the leisurely discourse between
them does much to justify Decoud's ensuing action, as
well as Antonia's lifelong and subsequent loss. *Nostromo* is
a better novel because of these additional "three drops of
water"; Conrad's high-flown lovers are easier to swallow
when less sweet.

Writing to Pinker on August 22, 1903, Conrad offers a
guarantee similar to Cora Crane's (with her assurance
that, in the case of Crane's death, she could finish *The
O'Ruddy*). He promises that he can meet the serial deadline for *Nostromo*. "If people want to begin printing say in
Septer you may let them safely—for you know that, at the
very worst, H. stands in the background (quite confidentially you understand)."[37] There is a curious *pudeur* here.
For one who had openly affixed his name to *The Inheritors*, which was in large part Ford's, Conrad seems anxious
to cover these tracks. I do not mean either that he took
credit where it was not due or refused to give it when it
was. But his pride in *Nostromo* might militate against such
sharing, just as his meticulousness would render him
uneasy. Ford's memory that he was "practically under
oath" squares with Conrad's assurance that he waits in the
background "quite confidentially you understand."

Something of the same appears in a letter explaining the
provenance of "One Day More" and why Ford extracted
the dialogue for the play from Conrad's short story
"Tomorrow." Here we may be dealing rather more with
other people's expectations than Conrad's own, and the
stereotypical image of the artist as a solitary. Conrad
wrote "One Day More" in Galsworthy's studio and parts of
Nostromo with Ford in the room. But the ivory tower has

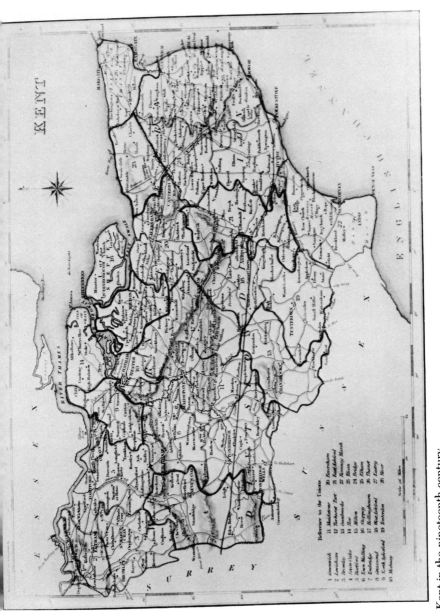

Kent in the nineteenth century

Above, photograph by H. G. Wells of himself and Conrad at Spade House, circa 1902, from *H. G. Wells: A Pictorial Biography*. (Courtesy Jupiter Books, Ltd.)

Below, manuscript of Ford Madox Ford's Preface to *Joseph Conrad: A Personal Remembrance*. (Courtesy Princeton University Library; the gift of Edward Naumberg, Jr.)

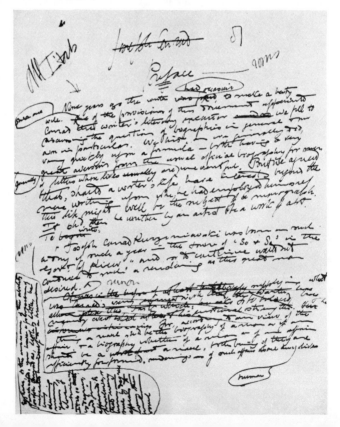

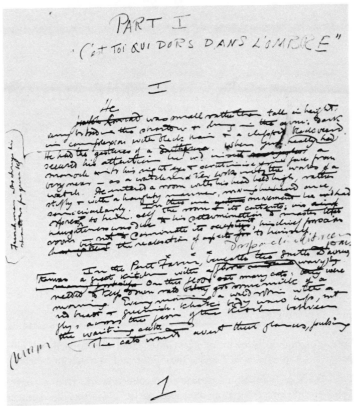

Above, manuscript of Ford Madox Ford's Part I (*"C'est toi qui dors dans l'ombre"*) of *Joseph Conrad: A Personal Remembrance*. (Courtesy Princeton University Library; the gift of Edward Naumberg, Jr.)

Below, Henry James eating a doughnut at the Brede Rectory garden fête, August 1899. (Stephen Crane Papers, Rare Book and Manuscript Library, Columbia University)

THE GHOST.

Written by

Mr. HENRY JAMES, Mr. ROBERT BARR,
Mr. GEORGE GISSING, Mr. RIDER HAGGARD,
Mr. JOSEPH CONRAD, Mr. H. B. MARRIOTT-
WATSON, Mr. H. G. WELLS, Mr. EDWIN PUGH,
Mr. A. E. W. MASON AND
Mr. STEPHEN CRANE.

BREDE SCHOOL HOUSE,

DECEMBER 28TH, 1899.

7.45 P.M.

DEACON, PRINTER, RYE

Above, autographed program of *The Ghost,* from the original in Columbia University. (Stephen Crane Papers, Rare Book and Manuscript Library)

Below left, Max Beerbohm's caricature recollection of "Henry James and Joseph Conrad conversing at an afternoon party." (Courtesy the Humanities Research Center, University of Texas at Austin, and Mrs. Eva Reichmann); *Right,* a caricature of Ford Madox Ford by W. Cotton. (The Bettmann Archive)

Left, signed photograph of H. G. Wells, circa 1897, from *H. G. Wells: A Pictorial Biography*. (Courtesy Jupiter Books, Ltd.)

Below, Joseph and Jessie Conrad visiting the Cranes in Ravensbrook, 1898. The Conrads stand in the doorway; Stephen Crane is holding a dog, and Cora holds the Conrad's eldest son, Borys. (Courtesy the Humanities Research Center, University of Texas at Austin)

Above, Henry James and Cora Crane at the Brede Rectory garden fête, August 1899. (Stephen Crane Papers, Rare Book and Manuscript Library, Columbia University)

Below, the last photograph of Stephen Crane alive, 1900, sitting in the garden at Brede Place with his dog, "Spongie." (Stephen Crane Collection, Clifton Waller Barrett Library, University of Virginia)

Above, building operations at Spade House, from H. G. Wells's *Experiment in Autobiography*, the Macmillan Company, New York.

Left, the present facade of Pent Farm; *Below left*, Brede Place in ruins; *Right*, Lamb House, seen from the garden. (Photographs by Nicholas Delbanco)

Sussex in the nineteenth century

been perceived to stand in splendid isolation; it looks like an office if shared.

All this is doubly astonishing in that Ford was no mimic; his ear for intonations other than his own had less than perfect pitch. He could and did produce a humorous pastiche of James, but the purpose of the novel's install- ment was to keep the presses going without hitch. As sug- gested above, the dialogue in the drawing room was very much within his competence. Ford's prose is recognizably his and not so similar to Conrad's. Yet the manuscript pages—with few corrections and composed on the run— confirm his claim that the installment was "a job that pre- sented no great difficulties to me." He is as much a secret sharer in *Nostromo* as when taking dictation for *A Mirror of the Sea*.

The chapter for *T. P.'s Weekly* may have taken both a conscious and conscientious effort to subordinate his sense of self, the idiosyncratic diction that asserts identity. Or the opposed identities may have, momentarily, merged. It shows the degree to which collaboration can forge prose parts into a seamless whole. As Conrad was fond of saying, and Ford proud to report, " 'By Jove . . . it's a third person who is writing!' "[38]

He said this in reference to the "welded collaboration" that resulted in three texts. As indicated, they began with the project of *Romance*, but this did not appear in print till 1903. Twenty years later, Conrad summarized their responsibilities in a letter to Ford:

I suppose our recollections agree. Mine, in their simplest form, are: First Part, yours; Second Part, mainly yours, with a little by me on points of seamanship and such like small matters; Third Part, about 60% mine with impor- tant touches by you; Fourth Part mine, with here and there an important sentence by you; Fifth Part practi-

cally all yours, including the famous sentence at which
we both exclaimed: "This is Genius", (Do you remember
what it is?) with perhaps half a dozen lines by me . . .[39]

The "famous sentence" which struck the two as uproari-
ous is " 'Excellency, a few goats . . .' " And the two do
seem to have revised each other's work with close attention. Ford demonstrates, in that portion of the manuscript
which he printed in the *Transatlantic Review*, that the
writing is "a singular mosaic of passages written
alternately."[40]

Before *Romance* appeared, however, they published
The Inheritors. Ford wrote the bulk of this strange book,
adapting the science-fiction format of Wells for the purpose of political allegory (including a portrait of Henry
James as Callan, the *littérateur*). Conrad was given the
principal credit, and in a letter to *The New York Times
Saturday Book Review*, he published this corrective:

> It might have been wished, too, that the fact of collabo-
> ration had been made more evident on the face of the
> notice. The book is emphatically an experiment in collab-
> oration; but only the first paragraph of the review men-
> tions "the authors" in the plural—afterward it seems as if
> Mr. Conrad alone were credited with the qualities of
> style and conception detected by the friendly glance of
> the critic.
>
> The elder of the authors is well aware how much of
> these generously estimated qualities the book owes to the
> younger collaborator . . .[41]

They also jointly wrote "The Nature of a Crime" and
published it pseudonymously in *The English Review* of
April and May 1909. This story is as different from *The
Inheritors* as *The Inheritors* is from *Romance*. Epistolary
and passionate, it heralds *The Good Soldier*—but without
the artistic control. It, too, may be labeled "emphatically

an experiment." The collective cognomen, Baron Ignatz von Aschendorf, was taken because both Ford and Conrad were contributors to the *Review*—and, one suspects, because neither of them was sufficiently proud of the text to acknowledge authorship. They seem to have forgotten its very existence until it was exhumed for separate publication.

Conrad wrote a preface to the reissued story in 1924; he glossed over old quarrels or assessed them as useful. When Ford was "pass[ed] the pen . . . in the hope that he may be moved to contradict me," he quarreled not with Conrad but the anticipated critic. He was fearful that:

> . . . some philologist of that Posterity for which one writes, might, in the course of his hyena occupations, disinter these poor bones and, attributing sentence one to writer A and sentence two to B, maul at least one of our memories. With the nature of *those* crimes one is only too well acquainted.[42]

In *A Personal Remembrance*, Ford gives an account of how he read aloud what would be the first scene of *The Inheritors*. Conrad called it "chic." "And as soon as the writer had let Conrad know that this was a novel, not a short story, he knew that he was in for another collaboration." Claiming that this "is the only discoverable passage with which Conrad notably interfered," Ford reproduces the interference in italics:

> I had looked at her before; now I cast a sideways, critical glance at her. I came out of my moodiness to wonder what type this was. *She had good hair, good eyes, and some charm.* Yes. And something besides—a something— a something *that was not an attribute of her beauty.* The modelling of her face was so perfect as to produce an effect of transparency, *yet there was no suggestion of frailness; her glance had an extraordinary strength of life.*

Her hair was fair and gleaming, her cheeks coloured as if a warm light had fallen on them from somewhere. She was familiar till it occurred to you that she was strange.[43]

He then reconstructs their discussion:

Do you not hear Conrad saying, "*Damn* Ford's women," putting in, "She had good hair, good eyes and, some charm." And do you not see the writer at twenty-six, hitching and fitching with "a something—a something—a something—" to get an effect of delicacy, and Conrad saying, "Oh, hang it all, do let's get some definite particulars about the young woman"?[44]

This may not be accurate verbatim, but it has the feel of interpolation—of one man looking over the other's shoulder while he writes. The youthful author of *The Shifting of the Fire* would have to be schooled in concreteness. Ford argued always, later, for specificity in description, and his sense of "definite particulars" may well have been engendered here. But close analysis of who wrote what is both beyond the scope of this study and beside its point; I wish neither to "disinter these poor bones" nor to "maul at least one" of the two. We may take this fourth variety of collaboration as proved. There is no squabble as to provenance—as to who engendered "Amy Foster" or if Ford provided a scene of *Nostromo*. Agreement is attested by their signatures. It is a larger version of the process of dictation: partners at work on one text.

The issue therefore becomes not what or how they did, but how well and to what effect. *The Inheritors* displays several approaches to the business of collaboration; Etchingham Granger, the book's protagonist, is by no means unequivocal. At first, when asked to do what Ford would elsewhere call "the literary dustings and sweepings" for an

eminent author, he refuses. The "great" and suspect
Callan:

> . . . was dignified, cordial; discussed his breakfast with
> gusto, opened his letters, and so on. An anaemic aman-
> uensis was taking notes for appropriate replies. How
> could I tell him that I would not do the work, that I was
> too proud and all the rest of it?[45]

Later, a more congenial character, Churchill, makes a
similar proposition:

> "After all, one cannot refuse to take what offers," he said.
> "Besides, your right man to do the work might not suit
> me as a collaborator."
> "It's very tempting," I said.
> "Why, then, succumb," he smiled.
> I could not find arguments against him, and I
> succumbed.[46]

Perhaps the most telling equivocation echoes a phrase
from *Lord Jim*. "On the one hand, I was 'one of us,' who
had temporarily strayed beyond the pale; on the other, I
was to be a sort of great author's bottle-holder."[47] These
extracts are representative; Etchingham Granger chafes at
the bit. It is only long after the fact of collaboration that
Ford views the process with pride. And here it is crucial,
again, to distinguish process from result; Ford repudiated
The Inheritors. In *A Personal Remembrance* he calls it "a
queer, thin book which the writer has always regarded
with an intense dislike. Or no, with hatred and dread
having nothing to do with literature. . . . The writer's dislike for the book began as soon as the last word was written . . ."[48]

That he and Conrad could literally forget "The Nature
of a Crime" is further evidence. The book is truncate if not
unfinished, and Conrad seems to have been responsible for

scuttling the project. Their friendship had grown strained. Ford used his affair with Violet Hunt as the subject of the story—a relationship Conrad deplored. The deep pattern of the piece has to do with betrayal, or at the least an abrogation of trust between business associates—and at the moment when the conflict between them went public in terms of *The English Review*. Conrad was unwilling to continue:

> I seem to remember a moment when I burst into earnest entreaties that all these people should be thrown overboard without more ado. This, I believe, *is* the real nature of the crime. Overboard. The neatness and dispatch with which it is done in Chapter VIII was wholly the act of my Collaborator's good nature in the face of my panic.[49]

So *Romance*, the project with which they began, remains the principal result. Entered into in good faith, it tried their faith at several junctures, and they each nursed doubts as to the merit of the book. Yet there was a kind of investment here (as well as the hope of financial return) that made them unwilling to quit. There is backbiting and hysteria—notably in Conrad's reaction to Ford's proposal that they date the work 1896–1903. He repudiates the notion that such an entertainment took two grown men six years to produce and urges that they confine the claimed production time to 1900–1902. "Or else put nothing."[50] This fussing with dates is symptomatic not only of Conrad's testiness but also his anxious integrity; he was working on *Nostromo* and knew the qualitative difference. That the work done in private was better is as true for Ford as Conrad, and that he recognized it as such. *The Good Soldier* would register as much of an advance over "The Nature of a Crime" as does *Nostromo* over *Romance*.

The question should therefore properly be: was the collaboration instrumental to their later, better work? I believe the answer to be yes.

This is easy to assert and difficult to prove. Not every apprentice becomes a master craftsman; if growth could be prescribed we all would improve all the time. And it is of course impossible to document what Conrad would have written had he not encountered Ford; quite possibly the master craftsman would have emerged nonetheless. But it must be remembered that Conrad, at the period of his move to Pent Farm, had written nothing comparable to what he produced thereafter. "The Nigger of the 'Narcissus,'" his major previous accomplishment, would not now be so widely read had he not continued to write. And even the famed preface has the ring of aspiration rather than attainment. He was serious, obviously, and committed to a career in prose, but as late as 1898 he spoke in his despondency of going back to sea. It is at least conceivable that had Ford not appeared on the scene—with his unstinting admiration and several varieties of support —Conrad would have quit.

More likely he would have continued. But the great creative decade comes so hard on the heels of their meeting that it is churlish to call it coincidence. Ford said as much, repeatedly, and this is where the seeming audacity of his claim most rankled. "I may as well dispose, once and for all, of the legend that I had any part in teaching Conrad English. . . ."[51] carries with it its own counterstatement. The "legend" that Ford here purports to dispose of was in large part generated by Ford. And though he goes to some length to qualify matters, he also says that he was the more sensitive to nuance and tone. This is, on the face of it, plausible enough. Yet he ascribes to Conrad the greater part of what might best be called conceptualization:

> We had the same aims and we had all the time the same aims. Our attributes were no doubt different. The writer probably knew more about words, but Conrad had certainly an infinitely greater hold over the architectonics of the novel, over the way a story should be built up so that its interest progresses and grows up to the last word.[52]

The theory of Impressionism seems to have been worked out in practice by the two together. Conrad probably took the lead at the time, and Ford promulgated the doctrine later. Neither of them as literary theorists holds a candle to James, but Conrad had a "European" concern for form. We need not call him the English Flaubert to call him the principal here. His summary of *Romance*, twenty years after publication, breaks the whole into component parts, and his novels of the period show conscious structuring.

All novels are consciously structured, of course, and distinction is a matter of degree. But the habit of mind that would recall *Romance* as a five-part venture is the same which would cast *Nostromo* into three. What Ford describes as "the architectonics of the novel" were clearly important to Conrad, even when he wrote for serial publication. And he would have influenced Ford. The shapeliness of Ford's books, beginning with *The Fifth Queen* trilogy and coming to fruition in *Parade's End*, goes somehow against their author's own grain. Ford seems most at ease when rambling, or with one of James's "baggy monsters"; his habitual mode is both discursive and digressive. His several reminiscences and travel texts (as well as the lesser novels) are anecdotal in the extreme; Dowell's stated method is that of the fireside chat.

Yet *The Good Soldier* is perfectly wrought. One of its triumphs comes from the tension established between the apparently casual discourse and the tautly reined-in and organized plot. This is perhaps why it is known as "the finest French novel in the English language." Told in a linear fashion, the tale of *The Good Soldier* would be little more than melodrama; it becomes "the saddest story" via its tortuous telling. The matter is simple enough, but the manner is impressively complex. Here it is tempting to discern the influence of Conrad's narrator, indirect discourse, and the theory of Impressionism; Ford's dedicatory note to the novel suggests a conscious fashioning of his "great auk's egg."

So, too, with the tetralogy: the formal exigency of *Parade's End* seems to me rather a decision taken than an instinctive response. This is another way of saying how much he owed to Conrad and their "welded collaboration." Because it is precisely such enforced attention to form that gives Ford's greatest work its power: the narrative vitality goes far beyond the strategies he employed earlier. If Conrad gained in fluency while working on *Romance*, Ford learned profluence.

At any rate, they improved. Neither of them would often again be so negligent as to write, "I may say that it was thanks to me that we reached the ship. Our boat went down under us whilst I was tying a rope under Carlos' arms . . ."[53] The drama inherent in action is absolutely absent from this passage; adventure comes as summary. Nor would Ford and Conrad often use again such fatuous phrasing as "We turned back, and the undulation of her walk seemed to throw me into a state of exaltation."[54] Whenever the figure of Seraphina sashays across its pages, *Romance* abounds in "undulation" and "exaltation." And their later dialogue, no matter how stilted, improves upon the following hodgepodge:

> I advise the señor to keep, now, within the Casa. No songs can give that vermin the audacity to seek the señor here. The gate remains barred; the firearms are always

loaded; and Cesar is a sagacious African. But methinks this moon would fall out of the heaven first before they would dare. . . . Keep to the Casa, I say—I, Tomas Castro.[55]

Ford gives an amusing account of Conrad's reaction to the first pages he read. They were deciding to collaborate on what was then *Seraphina*:

We began that reading after lunch of a shortish day; the lamps were brought in along with the tea. During that interval Conrad showed nervous and depressed; sunk in on himself and hardly answering questions. Conrad being then almost a stranger, this was the writer's first experience of to what Conrad's depression over an artistic problem could amount. . . . Conrad began to groan. . . . It was by then fairly apparent to the writer that Conrad disapproved of the treatment of the adventures of John Kemp, at any rate in Cuba; and the writer had a sufficient sense already of Conrad's temperament to be disinclined to ask whether his guest were ill. He feels now the sense of as it were dumb obstinacy with which he read on into those now vocal shadows in the fireside warmth. . . . The interruptions grew in length of ejaculation. They became, "O! O! . . . O God, my dear Hueffer . . ." . . . And towards the end, "O God, my dear *faller*, how is it possible. . . ."[56]

By the end of the collaboration, however, things improved:

. . . towards the end of our labours on those books, we had got so used to reading our own works aloud to each other that we finally wrote for the purpose of reading aloud the one to the other. That statement Conrad corroborated by passing it for the press—as it were with his dying breath. And that we should thus have written must have meant a similar taste in words, for it would be insupportable to have to listen, evening after evening, to prose that you did not like and almost as intolerable to read your own work to a person who did not like your turns of phrase.[57]

There is pathos in Ford's attempt to keep their friendship and its memory alive. Conrad became an unwilling and distant collaborator; the later overtures were almost entirely Ford's. The one who began the association terminated it also. Their final correspondence (with the notable exceptions instanced above) concerns itself with business; Conrad grew suspicious and aloof. As Frederick R. Karl indicates, the old competition may have revived—since Ford was flourishing as an artist by the time Conrad declined. It is intriguing to note that Ford's first major fictive efforts (*The Fifth Queen*, 1906; *Privy Seal*, 1907; and *The Fifth Queen Crowned*, 1908) came hard on the heels of the completion of *Romance*. Catherine Howard, the fifth wife of Henry VIII, is a closely seen and fully realized heroine; Ford wears his learning lightly. He also produced *The Benefactor* and *An English Girl* in that period, but the common denominator is a concentration on matters English and historical. *The Soul of London*, *The Heart of the Country*, and *The Spirit of the People* make up a kind of nonfiction trilogy on the theme of "Englishness." One could therefore argue—though Ford never did —that he was hunting independence, a terrain on which his Polish lordship could not poach.

Whatever the later constraints on their amity, they had been intimate once. In 1900, for instance, the families traveled together to Belgium. It was to have been a working vacation, with *Romance* on the shared drawing board —but the hotels were noisy and little Borys fell ill. Ford made himself useful in various ways, and one of the few paragraphs of Jessie's approval has to do with his function as nursemaid. She grants him competence with cold compresses and broth.

If only in the guise of nursemaid, Ford would have had function enough. But his roles were many and his contribution real; that Conrad flourished in his company has been, I hope, sufficiently shown. We need only compare a scene in *Nostromo* with its antecedent in *Romance* to read a record of growth. Decoud and Nostromo are becalmed on the gulf of Sulaco, as had been Kemp, Seraphina, and Tomas Castro in the fog. (A third and parallel instance is that of Jim on the immobilized *Patna*.) Conrad's characters follow somewhat pat patterns; his inventiveness is limited and his situations similar. This is true of every writer and therefore no indictment; the issue is what use he makes of a given quotient of material.

And I submit that Ford released the elder man to create profound scenarios by helping him to realize the surface of his texts. The opposition between surface and depth is a recurring theme in Conrad; *The Mirror of the Sea* reflects *The Shadow Line*. Captain MacWhirr of "Typhoon" "had sailed over the surface of the oceans as some men go skimming over the years of existence,"[58] and Peyrol of *The Rover* is similarly detached: "You have been the best part of your life skimming the seas. . . ."[59] The coastal vessel that brought coal from Newcastle to Lowestoft was called *Skimmer of the Sea*, as is Captain Hagberd's ship in "Tomorrow." And Alvan Hervey and his wife in "The Return" ". . . skimmed over the surface of life hand in hand . . . like two skillful skaters cutting figures on thick ice for the admiration of the beholders, and disdainfully ignoring the hidden stream, the stream restless and dark, the stream of life, profound and unfrozen."[60]

This "thick ice" and "the stream restless and dark" are two coordinates of Conrad's vision. And early on he plotted them with Ford. There was true reciprocity here. It is possible the two saved out the best part of invention in order to imagine such scenes once again and in private.

Yet this would have entailed a kind of conscious chariness and holding back for which there is no evidence in letter or memoir. When they were working on *Romance*, they worked as hard as they could. I think it more likely that Kemp in the fog becomes Decoud in the lighter by a process of association and enlargement impossible to trace. Impossible because unconscious and guarded and having to do with the alchemy in art—but possible to recognize by readers, once achieved.

The doctrine of Impressionism argues just such a practice in prose. It attempts to render surface facets as a painter or a sculptor might; it mimics the act of perception and forces the reader to follow the narrative "eye." Such a narrator is typically conscious and searching but confused; his memory is good but subject to evasion; his expectation as to behavior will be at odds with the discovered depths. So Kurtz can produce a high-minded pamphlet on the duties of the White Man when burdened with Colonials—then conclude with a single scrawled phrase, "Exterminate the brutes!" And Ashburnham, the model of an English gentleman, is scarcely what he seems. Progressive revelation will not merely show us more about a character, but more that is revealing in and of itself; we cannot know, at the beginning, all we will know at the end. The reader is a connoisseur and the page an object; he should study the surface of things.

This may seem both a truism and tautological. Every text can be described in equivalent terms. But the Impressionists were scrupulous—or sought to be—as to the distinction: what you see is what you see and must be shown as such. Therefore, Ford and Conrad argued for plasticity and that the modeling of contour in an incident merits close attention. Here they demonstrate with Marlow that ". . . the meaning of an episode was not inside like a kernel but outside, enveloping the tale which brought it out only as a glow brings out a haze . . ."[61] The Master Mariner as artist must plot his course with care; he must chart both the surface and depths.

The section of Ford's book on Conrad given over to their aesthetic takes its title from the latter's preface to "The Nigger of the 'Narcissus.'" Ford amplifies on Conrad's phrase "It is before all to make you see":

> We agreed that the general effect of a novel must be the general effect that life makes on mankind. A novel must therefore not be a narration, a report. . . . We saw that Life did not narrate, but made impressions on our brains. We in turn, if we wished to produce on you an effect of life, must not narrate but render impressions. . . . We agreed that the whole of Art consists in selection.[62]

He then adds to the categories of "General Effect," "Impressionism," and "Selection" subcategories of "Speeches" and "Conversations," with units on "Surprise" and "Style" as well as "Cadence," "Structure," "Philosophy," "*progression d'effet*" and "Language." All this is a little forced and considerably after the fact; it reports Ford's credo of 1924 at least as much as that of 1900. We have only his word for it that his collaborator employed such terminology. A quarter of a century later, Ford would codify what had been no doubt trial-and-error at the time.

But it does support the argument that the two men argued aesthetics and attempted to muster their own. The preface to "The Nigger"—written well before they met—evidences Conrad's preoccupation with "Art for Art's Sake" and the attempt to enlist a willing witness. We are all familiar with the challenge of conversation, the need to make articulate what are unspoken convictions—or with the process of discovering such convictions in speech. And it would have been plausible—unavoidable, even—that some such process took place with these two; they heard each other out.

It must have been something to hear. In his *Experiment in Autobiography*, Wells writes of Conrad with wit. There is an element of caricature in this description, but it gives the feel of foreignness and why Conrad would perhaps have fastened on "a very gifted scion of the Pre-Raphaelite stem":

> At first he impressed me, as he impressed Henry James, as the strangest of creatures. He was rather short and round-shouldered with his head as it were sunken into his body. He had a dark retreating face with a very carefully trimmed and pointed beard, a trouble-wrinkled forehead and very troubled dark eyes, and the gestures of his hands and arms were from his shoulders and very Oriental indeed. He reminded people of Du Maurier's Svengali and, in the nautical trimness of his costume, of Cutliffe Hyne's Captain Kettle. He spoke English strangely. Not badly altogether; he would supplement his vocabulary—especially if he were discussing cultural or political matters—with French words; but with certain oddities. He had learnt to read English long before he spoke it and he had formed wrong sound impressions of many familiar words; he had for example acquired an incurable tendency to pronounce the last *e* in these and those. He would say, "*Wat* shall we do with *thesa* things?" And he was always incalculable about the use of "shall" and "will."[63]

One final point about collaboration suggests a central paradox: too many cooks spoil the broth. This is in effect the generally accepted attitude, but it needs refining. And here the appropriate motto has to do with assiduity: if at first you don't succeed. . . . *The Inheritors* and "The

Nature of a Crime" were predominantly Ford's, and Conrad could not say of them what he wrote Henley about *Romance*—that "the material (is) of the kind that appeals to my imagination."

But to the degree that John Kemp's adventures did have such appeal, they may have deflected him from the shared story and into private reaches that would result in *Nostromo*. It takes no conscious chariness to know that a subject is worth repeating, and repetition can make the maker improve. So possibly the failure of a text may be more productive than success. Had Conrad not thrown "The Nature of a Crime" overboard, Ford might not have returned to it and salvaged *The Good Soldier*. This is conjecture again, but the short shrift accorded the one might well have afforded an impetus for the longer, more personal other. Ford says that he wrote *The Good Soldier*, at forty, in order to prove he could write one good book; the *ur*-text had not slaked that need.

That Ford profited from collaboration is beyond question; he says so himself and at length. A dilettante to start with, he became professional; the young and mannered dabbler grew to be "an old man mad about writing." His apprenticeship was served with Conrad, and the hierarchical aspects of life as a seaman may well have been germane. The captain found a responsive first mate. If Conrad's experience of English literature begins with Shakespeare's *Two Gentlemen of Verona*, his collaboration takes its epigraph from *King John*. This, as Ford recalls it, is the phrase:

> . . . nearly ideal literary friendships are rare, and the literary world is ennobled by them. It was that that Conrad meant when, looking up from the play of *King John* at which he had been glancing for a little while, he quoted to me, who was writing and had to turn my head over my shoulder to listen:

Oh, two such silver currents when they join
Do glorify the banks that bound them in—

And he added: *"C'est pas mal, ça; pour qualifier nous deux!"*[64]

IV.
James
and Wells

*The important point which I tried to argue
with Henry James was that the novel of
completely consistent characterization arranged beautifully in a story and painted
deep and round and solid, no more exhausts the possibilities of the novel, than
the art of Velasquez exhausts the possibilities of the painted picture.*

*The issue exercised my mind consider-
ably. I had a queer feeling that we were
both incompatibly right.*

   —H. G. Wells, *Experiment in
Autobiography,* 1934

IV.
James and Wells

Henry James's play *Guy Domville* had its opening night in London on January 5, 1895. It was not a success. Two days later, a reviewer for the *Pall Mall Gazette* observed that "the play was received with a marked disapproval by a considerable section of the audience." This is understatement; James was hissed. The "disapproval" came as a surprise. He walked out for his curtain call, hearing cries of "Author, author," and stood there while the praise was drowned out by abuse; he retained an anguished memory of having listened to "the hoots and jeers and catcalls of the roughs."[1]

James had stayed away from the performance. He was nervous, possibly, or modest; he attended Oscar Wilde's latest triumph instead of his own play. So he arrived too late to assess the audience reaction to *Guy Domville*. The manager may have been vengeful; there may have been a claque. James had misgivings, perhaps, but no notion of the débâcle to come or he would not have stepped out stage center. Nor had he much ability to weather such a storm; his skin was thin. He could not trade insults with the critics, as might have Wilde or Shaw. Twenty years earlier, James himself had prescribed hissing as a remedy for poor theater. The author and the actor should be disabused of pridefulness, he wrote, and made to hear abuse. In some sense this remedy worked. The dear dream of success "dropped from me in the twinkling of an eye," and James would never again expose himself in such a public fashion; at fifty-two he turned back from the theater to prose.

His humiliation was made the more complete, perhaps, because so many of his friends were there to witness it. Sir Edward Burne-Jones, Sir Frederick Leighton, John Singer Sargent, Mrs. W. K. Clifford, Mrs. Humphry Ward, the Terry sisters, Edmund Gosse, and George Du Maurier were but a few of the eminent artists who watched him stand, shake, and flee. H. G. Wells was not as yet eminent and not as yet a friend; it is he, however, who wrote the *Pall Mall Gazette* review. There is some praise in it; the play is "finely conceived and beautifully written." But the characteristic note in Wells—though his evening suit was three days old and this was his second assignment—is present already as challenge:

> . . . of all defects feebleness is the one most abhorred of the gods. The diagnosis points to an early deathbed; only a tonic treatment and the utmost gentleness on the part of those concerned in it can save the life of the play. . . . As it stands at present, the second act is hopeless, and the mental evolution of Guy Domville altogether incredible.[2]

Twenty years later, Wells launched a full-scale attack. Few satires can rival his *Boon*; the novelist hurls brickbats and parodies about him like a child in a tantrum, flailing.

There is range and sweep in the book, as well as excess; Wells took on the world of letters as if bent on braver new worlds. And once determined on a rupture with literary London, he determined it should be complete. A single quote suffices here to establish tone. One of *Boon's* principal targets is James:

> He spares no resources in the telling of his dead inventions. He brings up every device of language to state and define. Bare verbs he rarely tolerates. He splits his infinitives and fills them up with adverbial stuffing. He presses the passing colloquialism into his service. His vast paragraphs sweat and struggle; they could not sweat and struggle more if God himself was the processional meaning to which they sought to come . . . And all for tales of nothingness. . . . It is leviathan retrieving pebbles. It is a magnificent but painful hippopotamus resolved at any cost, even at the cost of its dignity, upon picking up a pea which has got into a corner of its den. Most things, it insists, are beyond it, but it can, at any rate, modestly, and with an artistic singleness of mind, pick up that pea . . .[3]

In 1895 Wells had signed the contract for but had not as yet published his first major success, *The Time Machine*; his audience would have been small. But in *Boon* his opinions were news, and others would write the reviews. *Boon* ended the friendship; the writers would not meet again. James's letters in rejoinder have a great deal of dignity; his eloquent correspondence served him better than did his silence after *Guy Domville*. And the twenty intervening years had of course altered them both.

The juxtaposition is nonetheless, I think, instructive. Wells first saw James in the context of public ridicule, and he last confronted James by ridiculing him in public. When the actor playing Guy pronounced, "Madame, I am the last of the Domvilles . . ." a voice from the gallery is supposed to have shouted, "And it's a bloody good thing you are." The echo would not have been conscious, but the enterprise of *Boon* is just such a shout from the gallery: a long, loud, witty hiss.

If the note of their association were uninterruptedly the catcall, however, we would not need to listen. James is easy enough to parody; few artists of our time have been so often caricatured. But James and Wells were friends, and close; until the final rupture they were never less than civil. Neither the circumstance of *Guy Domville* nor the attitude of *Boon* is representative. As Wells wrote in his autobiography, "I bothered him, and he bothered me . . . I had a queer feeling that we were both incompatibly right." The subject of this chapter is their closeness and their quarrel. It comes as counterpoint to the friendship of Conrad and Ford.

The claims and counterclaims are those of form and content; the problems were not new and have not been resolved. But that they should have been addressed by such intimate adversaries is, I think, unusual. In a letter to Hugh Walpole defending himself for *Boon*, Wells makes a telling connection:

> The James cult has been overdone. Anyhow nothing I've ever written or said or anyone has ever written or said about James can balance the extravagant dirtiness of Lubbock and his friends in boycotting Rebecca West's book on him in *The Times Literary Supplement*. My blood still boils at the thought of those pretentious academic greasers conspiring to down a friendless girl (who can write any of them out of sight) in the name of loyalty to literature.[4]

Wells was her friend—her lover, in fact—and, at this stage, loyal. There is much in Miss West's book that sounds like Wells himself. She was every bit his equal in the diatribe, and as keen a wit. The following extract from her *Henry James* is of a piece with *Boon*:

And it was peculiarly unfortunate that, while his subjects grew flimsier and his settings more impressive, his style became more and more elaborate. With sentences vast as the granite blocks of the Pyramids and a scene that would have made a site for a capital he set about constructing a story the size of a hen-house. The type of these unhappier efforts of Mr. James's genius is *The Sacred Fount* (1901), where, with a respect for the mere gross largeness and expensiveness of the country house which almost makes one write the author Mr. Jeames, he records how a week-end visitor spends more intellectual force than Kant can have used on *The Critique of Pure Reason* in an unsuccessful attempt to discover whether there exists between certain of his fellow-guests a relationship not more interesting among these vacuous people than it is among sparrows. The finely wrought descriptions of the leisured life makes one feel as though one sat in a beautiful old castle, granting its beauty but not pleased, because one is a prisoner, while the small, mean story worries one like a rat nibbling the wainscot.[5]

It is tempting to ascribe or to invent collusion here. It may even be that Wells and West, stung by James's refusal to sanction their affair, decided in some bed or bet that Henry was an animal. No man less plausible as beast, but a bestiary unfolds. This could have been purposive or coincidental, the agreement overt or covert. For James becomes—in the above quotations—a rat, leviathan, or hippopotamus; he builds hen house and pyramid with elephantine effort; he exalts a dead kitten or studies the behavior of sparrows.

These image clusters bespeak familiarity as well as contempt. It is a drawing-room comedy of sorts. Wells takes out after James because James will not take in Wells and West; West takes out after James, and Wells takes on those Jamesians who take out after West; James turns his face to the wall . . . There are scorned second parties and rejected suitors and sprightly ingenues and the stuff of farce; more seriously, there are questions of class, of public and private behavior, of bonds being broken or forged. Wells apologized after the fact:

> I had rather be called a journalist than an artist, that is the essence of it, and there was no other antagonist possible than yourself. But since it was printed I have regretted a hundred times that I did not express our profound and incurable difference and contrast with a better grace . . .[6]

James was not to be deflected. His magisterial response to Wells is both a credo and defense. The accusations rankled, having some of the sting of truth—having more importantly the ring of betrayal. His letter of July 10, 1915, begins by rejecting Wells's apology: "I am bound to tell you that I don't think your letter makes out any sort of case for the bad manners of *Boon*, as far as your indulgence in them at the expense of your poor old H. J. is concerned." And it ends with a classic assertion:

> Meanwhile I absolutely dissent from the claim that there are any differences whatever in the amenability to art of forms of literature aesthetically determined, and hold your distinction between a form that is (like) painting and a form that is (like) architecture for wholly null and void. There is no sense in which architecture is aesthetically "for use" that doesn't leave any other art whatever exactly as much so; and so far from that of literature being irrelevant to the literary report upon life, and to its being made as interesting as possible, I regard it as relevant in a degree that leaves everything else behind. It is art that *makes* life, makes interest, makes importance, for

our consideration and application of these things, and I know of no substitute whatever for the force and beauty of its process.[7]

Wells answered three days later, but his full text has not survived. He expresses bewilderment at James's formulation: "When you say 'it is art that *makes* life, makes interest, makes importance,' I can only read sense into it by assuming that you are using 'art' for every conscious human activity. I use the word for a research and attainment that is technical and special."[8]

This is the heart of the matter and the argument's pivot point. A champion of journalism—indeed, almost its inventor as it is practiced today—proclaims that he would rather be a journalist than an artist. And he finds "no other antagonist possible than yourself." James rejects the challenge. His final denial still stands: "If I were Boon I should say that any pretense of such a substitute is helpless and hopeless humbug; but I wouldn't be Boon for the world, and am only yours faithfully. Henry James."[9]

How had they come to this pass? Things started amicably. When James first came to call on Wells in 1898, it was with the intention of helping his new neighbor. He bicycled to New Romney along with Edmund Gosse, and they all took tea. Wells remarks that "the experience of later years has made me realize that in this way the Royal Literary Fund was making its enquiries about me . . ."[10] But he had money sufficient to start building Spade House, and would in any case have rejected a handout. The attention pleased him, however; the early exchanges are full of concerned *politesse*.

The letters from Wells to James are comparatively rare; those from James to Wells survive. The American tended to burn his papers, whereas the younger Englishman made a point of retention. So the record seems one-sided, as if the overtures come continually from James. Shortly after the failure of *Guy Domville*, James confessed to William Dean Howells: "I *have* felt, for a long time past, that I have fallen upon evil days—every sign or symbol of one's being in the least *wanted* anywhere or by any one having so utterly failed. A new generation, that I know not, and mainly prize not, has taken universal possession."[11] For James to make and prize the acquaintance of a leading member of the "new generation" was not therefore inconsequential. In 1898 he writes regarding Wells's health in the hope that "your convalescence bravely maintains itself." And he is full of fulsome apology that his visits are not more frequent. "Your so liberal and graceful letter is to my head like coals of fire—so repeatedly for all these weeks have I had feebly to suffer frustrations in the matter of trundling over the marsh to ask for your news and wish for your continued amendment . . ."[12]

This letter of December 9 contains an explanation of the methodology of James's "The Turn of the Screw." Wells evidently queried some point—a query to which James may have alluded in his later preface. But here he justifies his strategy and provides a schoolmasterly corrective to Wells's apparent misreading. He seems patient, avuncular: "Bless your heart, I think I could say worse of the T. of the S. . . . One knows the *most* damning things about oneself." And Wells answered, on January 16, 1899, with the kind of *mea culpa* that avows apprenticeship. He says he stands corrected:

> The story is not wrong—I was. My conversion was accompanied by the profound conviction of sin and culminated in the small hours. I came to Grace in this way. On the assumption that this story is wrong, it should be possible for the 'prentice even to indicate the right way. I had one or two walks and several hours by the fire, and a night (some time before the night of Grace) pursuing

the obvious remedy into blind alleys (where it van-
ished). Then it was resolved that the story was impossible and some convention had to be arranged. What was
the minimum convention possible? And so, to enlight-
enment.

I've had a profitable time and I shan't make such comments on your work again. It isn't at all a lovely story but
I treated it with a singularly vulgar lack of respect, and if
you were not a novelist I should doubt of your
forgiveness.[13]

By 1900 James is suggesting, cautiously, that Wells
might be more cautious in his prose. "You are very magnificent. I am beastly critical—but you are in a still higher
degree wonderful. I rewrite you much, as I read—which
is the highest praise my damned impertinence can pay to
an author."[14] He writes this of *The Time Machine* and,
some months later, says much the same of *Love and Mr.
Lewisham*. "I have found in it a great charm and a great
deal of the real thing—that is of the note of life, if not *all*
of it (as distinguished from the said great deal.) Why I
haven't found 'all' I will some day try and tell you: it may
be more feasible *viva voce* . . ."[15]

On September 23, 1902, James goes further still. He
makes a crucial offer—one which, if accepted, might well
have altered the history of Edwardian letters. Having read
Two Men, he writes:

It is, the whole thing, stupendous, but do you know what
the main effect of it was on my cheeky consciousness? To
make me sigh, on some such occasion to *collaborate* with
you, to intervene in the interest of—well, I scarce know
what to call it: I must wait to find the right name when
we meet. You can so easily avenge yourself by collaborat-
ing with *me!* Our mixture would, I think, be effective. I
hope you are thinking of doing Mars—in some detail. Let

me in *there*, at the right moment—or in other words at an
early stage . . .[16]

The italics are his. We have no record of Wells's answer,
but he must have expressed some surprise. Perhaps he
thought the offer was courteous merely, and replied in
kind. Possibly they did meet and James urged in conversation both his "interest" and rationale. For the offer was not
idle; James repeated it. They shared a literary agent—
James B. Pinker—and the senior author requests an
opportunity to work on Wells's manuscript (which would
be published as *Kipps*). His next letter is worth reproducing in full.

> LAMB HOUSE, RYE, SUSSEX.
> October 7, 1902.

My Dear Wells,

I feel that I should explain a little—even while I snatch
at and tenderly nurture to a possible maturity any germ
of interest and response in you. It is only that my sole
and single way of perusing the fiction of Another is to
write it over—even when most immortal—as I go. Write it
over, I mean, *re*-compose it, in the light of my own high
sense of propriety and with immense refinements and
embellishments. I am so good in these cases as to accept
the subject *tel quel*—to take it over whole and make the
best of it. I took over so, for instance, in my locked
breast, the subject of Two Men, etc. and the superstruc-
ture I reared upon it had almost no resemblance to, or
nothing in common (*but* the subject!) with yours. Unfortunately yours had been made public first—which seemed
hardly fair. To obviate this injustice I think (and to
secure an ideal collaboration) I should be put in possession of your work in its occult and pre-Pinkerite state.
Then I should take it up and give it the benefit of my
vision. After which—as post-Pinkerite—it would have
nothing in common with the suggestive sheets received

by me, and yet we should have labored in sweet unison. Think of it well—sending me on, even, at your early convenience of "Shy and Shocked or the Burden of the Bashful"—or whatever you think of calling the so enticing scheme you last hint at to me. Think of it, think of it; and believe me your faithful finisher,

Henry James[17]

Given James's reported horror at the collaboration taking place in Winchelsea and Postling ("To me this is like a bad dream which one relates at breakfast . . .") his offer to be Wells's "faithful finisher" is significant. Nothing came of it, of course; *Kipps* comes from Wells alone. And given James's habitual if tongue-in-cheek hyperbole ("You reduce me to mere gelatinous grovel," he once wrote Wells), his proposition might not have seemed in earnest. But I believe it was—at least as much so as Crane's was to Conrad that they write *The Predecessor*. James would neither have repeated nor elaborated on the offer had he not intended Wells to "think of it, think of it." His tone here is suitably self-mocking ("I am so good in these cases as to accept the subject *tel quel* . . ."); he makes light of without disguising the fact that "we should have labored in sweet unison."

Coming as it did from an established master of mandarin prose, and addressed to the colloquial Wells, it is a startling notion. And it was specific. James penned no general and pious wish that sometime in the future they might work together; he named the manuscript. He had heard Wells talk of *Kipps*, "the so enticing scheme," and wanted to deliver it from the problems that he found in *Love and Mr. Lewisham*. Such a collaboration might have challenged and changed them both. James engages in false modesty with his "immense refinements and embellishments." But his central phrase is direct: "Then I should take it up and give it the benefit of my vision." He stood ready to act as editorial conscience in, if not as literal co-author of, Wells's work. He wanted to *"write it over."*

In a sense James was to enact this procedure by and for himself later on. The New York edition of that work he chose to preserve is perhaps the most ambitious revision of a vision ever undertaken; it surely indicates his power of critical assessment and his willingness to *"re*-compose." Not many authors have the temperament for this sort of retentive attention; some cannot even open the pages of their printed books. James was peculiarly and particularly inclined to reconsideration, however. Once become a senior author, he afforded his own junior texts the scrutiny and "benefit of my vision" he here offers Wells. So we have a further if bizarre instance of collaboration between the youthful and the elder James; he precedes himself. Such an interpretation carries the notion of a "secret sharer" or artistic *doppelgänger* to a technically invalid extreme, since a single author cannot collaborate. But I find no disjunction in the proposal made to and refused by Wells and the proposition made and accepted by James later on; work should be reworked.

James's next preserved letter comes five weeks later—on November 15. By this time the tables have turned. Wells asked to see something of James's—perhaps in reciprocity, perhaps as a way of shifting the burden of proof. Conrad had seen a prospectus for James's *The Wings of the Dove.* And rumor of the notebooks was abroad—more particularly of the 20,000-word prospectus for *The Ambassadors.* Though completed by 1901, this novel had not yet appeared. So Wells requested the notes. Since we do not have his letter, we cannot determine its tone—whether he asked glancingly, in earnest, as a tender of his proposed collaborator's good intentions, or as a way of seeing how

James worked and if they could do so together. He had been told to "think of it"; he was doing so.

Yet James demurred. His answer begins: "It is too horribly long that I have neglected an interesting (for I can't say an interested) inquiry of yours—in your last note; and neglected precisely *because* the acknowledgement involved had to be an explanation." He then says the "*statements* (of my fictions that are to be) don't really exist in any form in which they can be imparted." The copies are elsewhere or lost. The statements have produced too little, and:

> I shall not again draw up detailed and explicit plans for unconvinced and ungracious editors; so that I fear I shall have nothing of that sort to show. A plan for *myself*, as copious and developed as possible, I always do draw up —that is the two documents I speak of were based upon, and extracted from, such a preliminary *private* outpouring. But this latter voluminous effusion is, ever, so extremely familiar, confidential and intimate—in the form of an interminable garrulous letter addressed to my own fond fancy—that, though I always, for easy reference, have it carefully typed, it isn't a thing I would willingly expose to any eye but my own. And even *then*, sometimes, I shrink! So there it is. I am greatly touched by your respectful curiosity, but I haven't, you see, anything coherent to produce.[18]

However James glosses it over, he is here rejecting Wells's request. The effusions have been "carefully typed," but the answer is no. The true collaborator should have access to "a preliminary *private* outpouring" also; it was this, indeed, that James had asked of Wells. And the italics stressing privacy are his.

James's editors have furnished us, after his death, what his friends could not read at the time. Posterity in this case acts as Peeping Tom. We see what Wells was prevented from seeing—the notebooks or "letter addressed to my own fond fancy." His prospectus for *The Ambassadors* is scarcely a private document, and his revulsion from "unconvinced and ungracious editors" had nothing to do with Wells. His sense of public failure (he was latterly unable to place his work in magazines and to publish the novels serially) may have held him back. To be fair, James was often thus reticent; he destroyed many of his letters and much manuscript. He had a horror of the kind of personal confession that would later empower Wells's *Experiment in Autobiography*; he had intended, perhaps, no closer an association than that which linked their names on the program of *The Ghost*.

Still, the offer to Wells was one-sided. And it may have seemed like condescension, as if the *primus inter pares* here asserted primacy. Collaboration cuts both ways. If Wells would refuse the aid of the Royal Literary Fund, and had seemed so self-sufficient that they did not even offer it, why should he thereafter accept the advice of one who offered instruction? As James admits a year later, the fame of the newcomer far outstripped—in commercial terms, at least—his own. On October 14, 1903, and referring to Wells's praise of *The Ambassadors*, he writes:

> It's a luxury to be read with a certain intelligence—and the quality must make up for the quantity. My book has been out upwards of a month and, not emulating your 4,000, has sold, I believe, to the extent of 4 copies. In America it is doing better—promises to reach 400. But I count your letter as, for a result, at least a thousand. . . .[19]

Soon thereafter, James seeks Wells's advice. He would like to increase his sales in America. James complains of Pinker's inefficacy and sighs for Wells's acumen and dash.

This letter is dictated; it seems more businesslike. The tone of their exchange alters perceptibly now. It is more intimate because longer-lasting; they have been correspondents for years. But the deep, shared trust and enthusiasm appear to wane; the familiarities appear conventional. Wells is an increasingly public presence, and James increasingly arcane. His reactions to Wells's "agglomerated lucubrations" edge almost to the point of mockery—though with a grace note of self-mockery also. James is full of praise but tortuous; the very excess of his enthusiasm suggests, somehow, something withheld.

Chapman and Hall published Wells's *The Future of America* in 1906; the next year they would publish James's *The American Scene*. As companion texts they offer marked comparisons; the former is prescriptive, the latter descriptive. In part, this derives from Wells's vocation as prophet, whereas James was elegiac about his native land. But two less similar texts can scarcely be imagined. Since the subject matter of these books is ostensibly one and the same, the separate treatments show how separate are the writers. Focus differs, as does tone; the voyagers arrive at polar "new found lands." James's response to Wells's presentation copy is fretful:

> This amounts to saying that what primarily flies in my face in *these* things of yours is *you* and your so amazingly active and agile intellectual personality—I may even say your sublime and heroic cheek—which I can't resist for the time, can't *sufficiently* resist, to allow me to feel (as much as I want to,) that you tend always to simplify overmuch (that is as to large *particulars*—though in effect I don't think you do here as to the whole.) But what am I talking about, when just this ability and impulse to simplify—so vividly—is just what I all yearningly envy you? —I who was accursedly born to touch nothing save to complicate it.[20]

*　*　*

One further private refusal here appears germane. By 1912 Wells was world-famous; the Royal Society of Literature invited him to join their Academic Committee. James was a member; so were such men as Conrad, Galsworthy, Hardy, Shaw, and Yeats. For years and by his own admission, Wells had courted the approval of just such men as these; they gave it sparingly. *Tono-Bungay*, in 1909, had been his most serious effort at "Art for Art's Sake"—but even there the frame kept getting confused with the picture. In 1911 Wells admitted an antipathy to the world of letters; he published an essay, "The Contemporary Novel," in which he took the literary establishment to task. (Later he was to change his mind and join P.E.N. International, becoming its president after John Galsworthy. But he did this much more for political purposes than as an occasion to argue aesthetics; in the face of Nazi and Communist repression, he hoped P.E.N. could help keep writers free.) In 1912 he was still young, however, still formulating this stance. He refused the invitation, and Edmund Gosse asked Henry James to tender it again. James did so, gracefully:

> On hearing of your election I felt a greater pleasure than anything in my connection with the body had yet given me, and if you maintain your refusal I shall continue, in pain and privation, to yearn for you. So I am moved to try respectfully to contend with you to some good issue on the subject . . . Don't make too much of rigours and indifferences, of consistencies and vows; I have no greater affinity with associations and academies than you —*a priori*; and yet I find myself glad to have done the simple, civil, social *easiest* thing in accepting my election —touched by the amenity and geniality of the thought that we shall probably *make something* collectively—in addition to what we may make individually. Don't think I want to harass or overbear you if I say that if these

words still leave you cold I frankly don't want to let the matter go without seeing you over it . . .[21]

Wells was equally graceful, but firm. Writing from Hampstead, on March 25, 1912, he replied:

My Dear James,

Your letter is most difficult to answer because I am not going to do as you wish. It's most difficult because not only have I a very deep affection for you but I have that snobbishness towards you which is quite honourable. I do look up to, and admire, and feel proud of my connexion with your beautiful fine abundant mind—I like to be about with you and in the same boat with you. If it was only you—. But I have an insurmountable objection to Literary or Artistic Academies as such, to any hierarchies, any suggestion of controls or fixed standards in these things. I feel it so strongly that indeed I would rather be outside the Academic Committee with Hall Caine, than in it with you and Gosse and Gilbert Murray and Shaw. This world of ours, I mean the world of creative and representative work we do, is I am convinced best anarchic. Better the wild rush of Boomster and the Quack than the cold politeness of the established thing. . . .[22]

He ended as follows: "Forgive this—the only word to express my feelings is—disobedience, and believe me/ Always yours." The feel of the renegade is strong throughout, and Wells's sense of loss attached to "disobedience." "I like to be about with you and in the same boat with you. If it was only you—" might even refer to *Kipps* and their failed chance at collaboration. In his letter of January 16, 1899, Wells promised, "I shan't make such comments on your work again." But the "world . . . best anarchic" would give him license; his "insurmountable objections to . . . any suggestion of controls or fixed standards" puts his position clearly.

James tried once more, however. He answered by return mail:

> I know perfectly what you mean by your indifference to Academies and Associations, Bodies and Boards, on all this ground of ours; no one should know better, as it is precisely my own state of mind—really caring as I do for nothing in the world but lonely patient virtue, which doesn't seek that company . . . Your plea of being anarchic and seeing your work as such isn't in the least, believe me, a reason against; for (also believe me) you are essentially wrong about that! No talent, no imagination, no application of art, as great as yours are, is able not to make much less for anarchy than for a continuity and coherency much bigger than any disintegration. There's no representation, no picture (which is your form) that isn't by its very nature preservation, association, and of a positive associational *appeal*—that is the very grammar of it; none that isn't thereby some sort of interesting or curious *order*: I utterly defy it in short not to make, all the anarchy in the world aiding, far more than it unmakes. . . . So it is that you are *in* our circle anyhow you can fix it, and with us always drawing more around (though always at a respectful and considerate distance,) fascinatedly to admire and watch.[23]

Wells came to the Reform Club the next day, found James at lunch, and repeated his refusal. In a note to Edmund Gosse, James concludes the business. He recognizes how far Wells has traveled from the center of that "circle," and how the enterprise of art appears merely tangential to his junior colleague now:

> I had a good deal of talk with him—though not, his refusal once perfectly *net*, about that, and without his having answered or met in any way any one of the things my second letter (any more for that matter than any of those my first) had put to him; and my sense that he is right about himself and that he wouldn't at all do among

us from the moment our whole literary side—or indeed
any literary side anywhere—is a matter of such indifference to him as I felt it to be today—to an extent I hadn't
been aware of. He has cut loose from literature clearly—
practically altogether; he will still do a lot of writing
probably—but it won't be *that*. This settles the matter,
and I now agree with you settles it fortunately. He *had*
decently to decline, and I think it decent of him to have
felt that.[24]

The inference is now no longer hidden; Wells is in open
rebellion. James covers his own tracks a little, saying
Wells could have answered his points. But the conclusion
of his second plea enjoins this very dialogue: "Don't
answer or acknowledge this unless it may have miracu-
lously moved you by some quarter of an inch." Wells *did*
come to the club for lunch, but for a different reason. "I
think he came on purpose to find me," James writes Gosse,
"and let me see that he is absolutely immovable . . ." One
does not need to read these notes as stage directions for a
parable of disobedience or filial revolt in order to see,
here, how intimate the adversaries were and how much it
pained them to elect their so separate camps. There is
petulance in James's summary, a little, but mostly a re-
signed recognition: "Wells wouldn't at all do among us.
. . . He *had* decently to decline." They knew they were in
opposition, and that the issue was joined.

"Mr. Pember's Academy," as Samuel Hynes refers to it,
has an interesting history. Modeled on the Académie
Française, and dedicated to the propositions that art is a
noble calling and excellence should be honored, it nonetheless ran counter to the deeper English attitudes that art
is but a business and excellence in flux. Wells's refusal carried the day. The Academy was first proposed in the
1890's. (Stephen Crane, as we have seen, had no use for
the idea of an American equivalent; he suggested that a

photogenic author be the single member.) The group took up its function in 1909 and was disbanded thirty years thereafter. The best attended meeting of the later years was the one which voted to disband. "The cold politeness of the established thing," as Wells describes it, had more to do with the Edwardian notion of stability than the reality of change. In *Tono-Bungay* and the career of Edward Ponderevo, Wells evokes "the wild rush of Boomster and the Quack." His vivid phrase is prototypical: it held true in journalism with the advent and ascendancy of Alfred Harmsworth; it feels more representative of this kinetic culture than does a formal elected assembly of "immortals" yet to die. . . . The friendship of our novelists had been in part predicated on their early distance from the center of the London literary scene, with its brokerage and ballyhoo; in this regard Wells was consistent.

Novelists will sooner or later commit their opinions to print. Their disagreement as to the Academy was a partly public one—more so, certainly, than earlier demurrals at the prospect of collaboration. It entailed third parties (Gosse *et al.*) and the problem of a group. So the dispute was bound to go public. In 1911, and with Wells's talk on "The Contemporary Novel," it did. Wells compliments Conrad; he makes no mention of James. He states that he has been thinking about novels for twenty years—since his first review of *Almayer's Folly*—and come to some conclusions. The novel is, he proposes, an instrument for the amelioration of the people's lot. "And this is where the value and opportunity of the modern novel comes in. So far as I can see, it is the only medium through which we can discuss the great majority of the problems which are being raised in such bristling multitude by our contemporary social development."

The essay began as a speech. And it retains the feel of

hortatory address, as if Wells were attempting to convince his literary confreres of the manifold utility of books. He ends with a call to art arms:

You see now the scope of the claim I am making for the novel; it is to be the social mediator, the vehicle of understanding, the instrument of self-examination, the parade of morals and the exchange of manners, the factory of customs, the criticism of laws and institutions and of social dogmas and ideas. It is to be the home confessional, the initiator of knowledge, the seed of fruitful self-questioning. Let me be very clear here. I do not mean for a moment that the novelist is going to set up as a teacher, as a sort of priest with a pen, who will make men and women believe and do this and that. The novel is not a new sort of pulpit; humanity is passing out of the phase when men *sit under* preachers and dogmatic influences. But the novelist is going to be the most potent of artists, because he is going to present conduct, devise beautiful conduct, discuss conduct, analyse conduct, suggest conduct, illuminate it through and through. He will not teach, but discuss, point out, plead, and display. And this being my view you will be prepared for the demand I am now about to make for an absolutely free hand for the novelist in his choice of topic and incident and in his method of treatment; or rather, if I may presume to speak for other novelists, I would say it is not so much a demand we make as an intention we proclaim. We are going to write, subject only to our limitations, about the whole of human life. We are going to deal with political questions and religious questions. We cannot present people unless we have this free hand, this unrestricted field. What is the good of telling stories about people's lives if one may not deal freely with the religious beliefs and organizations that have controlled or failed to control them? What is the good of pretending to write about love, and the loyalties and treacheries and quarrels of men and women, if one must not glance at those varieties of physical temperament and organic quality, those deeply passionate needs and distresses from which half the storms of human life are brewed? We mean to deal with all these things . . .[25]

It is an eloquent plea and impressively phrased. Yet one wonders what sort of teacher would fail to "discuss, point out, plead and display." No matter how uncertain in his early period, Wells's art was didactic—and, later, explicitly so. The assumption of the didact (particularly, perhaps, if he has been, as was Wells, an autodidact and a success story) is meliorist: things can get better and do. Conrad put it succinctly. He told Wells, "The difference between us is fundamental. You don't care for humanity but think they are to be improved. I love humanity but know they are not."[26]

James's first public discussion of Wells's work came in "The Younger Generation." A two-part article that appeared in *The Times Literary Supplement* of March 19 and April 2, 1914, it repeats what James's letters had urged. He picks a startling simile:

What we recognize the author as doing is simply recording his possession or, to repeat our more emphatic term, his saturation; and to see him as virtually shut up to that process is a note of all the more moment that we see our selected cluster of interesting juniors, and whether by his direct action on their collective impulse or not, embroiled, as we venture to call it, in the same predicament. They squeeze out to the utmost the plump and more or less juicy orange of a particular acquainted state and let this affirmation of energy, however directed or undirected, constitute for them the "treatment" of the theme.[27]

The author referred to above is Arnold Bennett. But James places Wells in the same fruit bin and uses the "orange" image repeatedly. He prods and plucks and squeezes and picks at their work like a finicky shopper with second-rate produce: it would have been surprising had Wells *not* taken offense. Twenty years before, James had written Howells that he neither knew nor prized "the younger generation"—but in the intervening years he showered Wells with praise. The echo of those private panegyrics can be heard here, but it is faint and far away; what comes through uninflected is his irritation:

If Mr. Bennett's tight rotundity, then, is of the handsomest size and his manipulation of it so firm, what are we to say of Mr. Wells's, who, a novelist very much as Lord Bacon was a philosopher, affects us as taking all knowledge for his province and as inspiring in us to the very highest degree the confidence enjoyed by himself?—enjoyed, we feel, with a breadth with which it has been given no one of his fellow-craftsmen to enjoy anything. If confidence alone could lead utterly captive we should all be huddled in a bunch at Mr. Wells's heels, which is indeed where we *are* abjectly gathered, so far as that force does operate. It is literally Mr. Wells's own mind, and the experience of his own mind, incessant and extraordinarily various, extraordinarily reflective, even with all sorts of conditions made, of whatever he may expose it to, that forms the reservoir tapped by him, that suffices for his exhibition of grounds of interest. The more he knows and knows, or at any rate learns and learns— the more, in other words, he establishes his saturation— the greater is our impression of his holding it good enough for us, such as we are, that he shall but turn out his mind and its contents upon us by any free familiar gesture and as from a high window forever open (Mr. Wells having as many windows as an agent who has bought up the lot of the most eligible to retail for a great procession).[28]

It is neither ingenious nor reading more than James

intended into the phrase ("turn out his mind and its contents upon us . . . as from a high window") to suggest that what Wells drops is garbage. That "free familiar gesture" belongs to Grub Street, and those who huddle "in a bunch at Mr. Wells's heels" cannot be other than dogs. These are not comparisons that keep a friend a friend.

Ford and Conrad urged control, calling it *progression d'effet*. They preferred the inner coherence of things to the marshaling of facts. James, writing of Wells's *Marriage*, finds neither control nor coherence. "We see effect, invoked in vain, simply stand off unconcerned; effect not having been at all consulted in advance, she is not to be secured on such terms. And her presence would so have redounded—perfectly punctual creature that she is on a made appointment and a clear understanding—to the advantage of all concerned."[29]

In his autobiography Wells concedes the point. More than twenty years after the fact, he says that James's objections to *Marriage* were proper but irrelevant:

> Henry James was quite right in saying that I had not thought out these two people to the pitch of saturation and that they did not behave unconsciously and naturally. But my defence is that it did not matter, or at least for the purposes of the book it did not matter very much. . . . And the only point upon which I might have argued but which I did not then argue, was this, that the Novel was not necessarily, as he assumed, this real through and through and absolutely true treatment of people more living than life. It might be more and less than that and still be a novel . . .[30]

This is a distinction of degree, not kind; the French *sensible* is cognate but opposed to the English "sensible." We might divide our novelists in the terms of preference: James would have endorsed the former pronunciation,

Wells the latter. In terms of "sensibility," this is "the whole contention." Virginia Woolf and Arnold Bennett engaged in just such wrangling, and it scarcely needs repeating that we are contentious still. *Sensible* in French translates to "sensitive"; "sensible" in English usage means possessed of "common sense."

In his autobiography Wells reconsiders the closing sentences of "The Contemporary Novel." He restates his position, then demurs:

> These are brave trumpetings. In effect in my hands the Novel proved like a blanket too small for the bed and when I tried to pull it over to cover my tossing conflict of ideas, 1 found I had to abandon questions of individuation. I never got "all life within the scope of the novel." (What a phrase! Who could?)[31]

But these disclaimers do not qualify the claim. Wells had grown impatient with James's strictures and restrictions, and that impatience grew. He wrote his fiction "lightly and with a certain haste"; he admitted to this without shame.

Perhaps the most revealing of his several letters to James in this period dates from September 22, 1913. It is cheerful, unabashed; it advertises its unconcern. James had dealt, the day before, with Wells's *The Passionate Friends;* his praise-cum-complaint must have seemed familiar. He had written *The Reverberator*, after all, and was no stranger to journalism; he makes use of Wells's metaphor ("I like to be about with you and in the same boat . . ."):

> I find you perverse and I find you, on a whole side, unconscious, as I can only call it, but my point is that *with* this heart-breaking leak even sometimes so nearly playing the devil with the boat your talent remains so savoury and what you do so substantial. I adore a

rounded objectivity, a completely and patiently achieved one, and what I mean by your perversity and your leak is that your attachment to the autobiographic form for the *kind of thing* undertaken, the whole expression of actuality, "up to date," affects me as sacrificing what I hold most dear, a precious effect of *perspective*, indispensable, by my fond measure, to beauty and authenticity. Where there needn't so much be question of that, as in your hero's rich and roaring impressionism, his expression of his own experience, intensity and avidity as a whole, you are magnificent, there your ability prodigiously triumphs and I grovel before you.[32]

Wells's answer is immediate. It blends gratitude with mockery:

My Dear James,

You are the soul of generosity to me. That book is *gawky*. It's legs and arms and misfitting clothes. It has spots like an ill grown young man. Its manners are sly and clumsy. It has been thrust into the world too soon. I shall now be an artist. (The image alters here.) My art is abortion—on the shelves of my study stand a little vaingloriously—thirty-odd premature births. Many retain their gill slits. The most finished have still hare lips, cleft palates, open crania. These are my children! But it is when you write to me out of your secure and masterly *finish*, out of your golden globe of leisurely (yet not slow) and infinitely *easy* accomplishment that the sense of my unworthiness and rawness is most vivid. Then indeed I want to embrace your feet and bedew your knees with tears—of quite unfruitful penitence.

Yours ever,
H. G. Wells[33]

The Prodigal Son, returning, says, "Father, I have sinned and am not worthy to be called thy son." There is at least a mime of that gesture and an echo of that speech in Wells's "sense of my unworthiness . . . I want to embrace your feet." Yet the mime and the gesture ("bedew your knees with tears . . .") edge up to a burlesque. For he knows the penitence will prove unfruitful; he is in fact impenitent. James must have been shocked by the ghoulish humor of "My art is abortion," and the tropes that follow; Wells writes "a little vain-gloriously" about his "thirty-odd premature births." When he promises that "I shall now be an artist," his promise is scarcely heartfelt, and the italics and parenthetical observations mock James's own. He thumbs his nose at instruction with "The image alters here."

James's garden room was destroyed in the Second World War. His personal effects have been sold, and only a few books remain behind glass. Of the cabinet of presentation copies thus preserved in Lamb House, two are by Wells. The first, in 1908, *New Worlds for Old*, is inscribed with the prodigal's question: "But will your charity reach so far?" In 1914 Wells produced another trumpet blast in favor of modernity. *The World Set Free* has the witty and tongue-in-cheek inscription "These squeezings." A clear reference to James's evocation of "a plump and more or less juicy orange," the formula contrives to be both arrogant and modest. Whether James read or what he made of these two offerings is not, however, on record.

I have followed, roughly, a chronological progression here. But if the cart has seemed to come before the horse —if Wells appears to answer, in 1911, an observation James would make in an essay one year later—that is at least in part a function of anachrony. The egg has been hatching the chicken since *Guy Domville* and their first encounter. Let us take one more example. After his broadside appeared, Wells wrote to James, "Boon is just a waste-paper basket. Some of it was written before I left my house at Sandgate, and it was while I was turning over some old papers that I came upon it. . . ."[34]

James answered as follows: "Your comparison of the book to a waste-basket strikes me as the reverse of felicitous, for what one throws into that receptacle is exactly what one *doesn't* commit to publicity and make the affirmation of one's contemporaries by. I should liken it much rather to the preservative portfolio or drawer in which what is withheld from the basket is savingly laid away . . ."[35] Yet one year earlier, in public, James had described Wells as doing just this—turning "out his mind and its contents upon us by any free familiar gesture."

It is not easy to justify *Boon*. Subtitled *The Mind of the Race, The Wild Asses of the Devil, and The Last Trump*, the book is a grab bag if not a wastepaper basket. But I have tried to suggest that the attack was neither random nor—from Wells's vantage—unprovoked. Condescension of the sort expressed by James would sooner or later elicit Wells's aggrieved response. (Something of the same had been the case in his relation to the Fabian Society, and to G. B. Shaw. The two had disagreed as to the function of their group; Shaw won the debate, Wells quit. *The Outlook for Homo Sapiens* and *The Mind at the End of its Tether* follow a similar pattern. Here the act of repudiation is self-reflexive; Wells denies at the end of his life those doctrines he had spent his life attempting to propound. The meliorist gives way to him who had envisioned the Morlocks as long ago as in *The Time Machine*. Some of Wells's later behavior verges on the paranoiac; he had fits of prideful suspicion and turned his back on several who were nearer and dearer than James. Such an interpretation would make of *Boon*—as indeed it proved to be with reference to the author as conscious artist—an act of self-destruction. A letter of October 19, 1912, demonstrates this double strain in Wells. Civility and real respect mingle with offhandedness. The diction signals a man of two minds. After the second sentence, his tone modulates; he calls his book "mixed pickles" and himself a whore:

My Dear James,

I am glad to think you are a little better and distressed to think there should be a *bad* from which the better has to come. And it is beyond measure good of you to give attention to my book and to mingle as you do so much heartening kindliness with the wisest, most penetrating and guiding of criticism and reproof. I am, like so many poor ladies, destined to be worse before I am better; the next book is "scandalously" bad in form, mixed pickles and I know it. It is I hope a prolonged acute disease rather than a chronic decay, and hereafter I will seek earnestly to make my pen lead a decent life, pull myself together, think of Form.

I hope very earnestly for your recovery. The *Reform Club* is a poor place without you.

Yours ever,
H. G. Wells[36]

Boon in the following discusses these matters with his friend, Dodd. Couched as dialogue—though very much a monologue—this extract gives Wells's answer to James's recent public utterance. He argues for the novel with "all life within . . .":

"But James *begins* by taking it for granted that a novel is a work of art that must be judged by its oneness. Judged first by its oneness. Some one gave him that idea in the beginning of things and he has never found it out. He doesn't find things out. He doesn't even seem to want to find things out. You can see that in him; he is eager to accept things—elaborately. You can see from his books that he accepts etiquettes, precedences, associations, claims. That is his peculiarity. He accepts very readily and then—elaborates. He has, I am convinced, one of the strongest, most abundant minds alive in the whole world, and he has the smallest penetration. Indeed, he has no penetration. He is the culmination of the Superficial type. Or else he would have gone into Philosophy and been greater even than his wonderful brother. . . . But here he is, spinning about, like the most tremendous of water-boatmen—you know those insects?—kept up by surface tension. As if, when once he pierced the surface, he would drown. It's incredible. A water-boatman as big as an elephant. I was reading him only yesterday—'The Golden Bowl'; it's dazzling how never for a moment does he go through."

"Recently he's been explaining himself," said Dodd.

"His 'Notes on Novelists.' It's one sustained demand for the picture effect. Which is the denial of the sweet complexity of life, of the pointing this way and that, of the spider on the throne. . . . But James sets out to make his novels with the presupposition that they can be made continuously relevant. And perceiving the discordant things he tries to get rid of them. He sets himself to pick the straws out of the hair of Life before he paints her. But without the straws she is no longer the mad woman we love. He talks of 'selection,' and of making all of a novel definitely *about* a theme. He objects to a 'saturation' that isn't oriented. And he objects, if you go into it, for no clear reason at all . . ."[37]

It is beyond this study's scope to piece together or parse the truth of Wells's assertion that "some of it [*Boon*] was written before I left my house at Sandgate." If indeed he pilloried James in 1905, before moving to town, he had remained politic for a decade. More likely he kept notes —perhaps even a section of the parody—and recurred to them in irritation when returned to *Boon*. But such questions as "Ought there to be such a thing as a literary

artist?" would not have presented themselves to Wells
when in the circle at Rye. And Boon's answer to a question, "Ought there, in fact, to be Henry James?" is
emphatic: "I don't think so."

Wells dismisses Hueffer (Ford) in passing. He invites
the younger author to a garden party, then sends him
swiftly packing:

> I remember how Boon sat on the wall of his vegetable
> garden and discoursed upon James, while several of us
> squatted about on the cucumber-frames and big flower-
> pots and suchlike seats, and how over the wall Ford
> Madox Hueffer was beating Wilkins at Badminton. Huef-
> fer wanted to come and talk too; James is one of his
> countless subjects—and what an omniscient man he is
> too!—but Wilkins was too cross to let him off . . .
>
> So that all that Hueffer was able to contribute was an
> exhortation not to forget that Henry James knew Turge-
> nev and that he had known them both, and a flat denial
> that Dickens was a novelist. This last was the tail of that
> Pre-Raphaelite feud begun in *Household Words*, oh! gen-
> erations ago . . .
>
> "Got you there, my boy!" said Wilkins. "Seven, twelve."
> We heard no more from Hueffer.[38]

James takes rather longer to dispatch. In a burlesque of
the mandarin style, Wells offers James's "agglomerated
lucubrations" (the term had been James's of Wells) on the
topic that had vexed them both:

> Why, in short, attempt to a comprehensiveness that
> must be overwhelming when in fact the need is for a
> selection that shall not merely represent but elucidate
> and lead. Aren't we, after all, all of us after some such
> indicating projection of a leading digit, after such an in-
> sistence on the outstandingly essential in face of this
> abundance, this saturation, this fluid chaos that perpetu-
> ally increases? Here we are gathering together to cele-

brate and summarize literature in some sort of undefined
and unprecedented fashion, and for the life of me I find
it impossible to determine what among my numerous
associates and friends and—to embrace still larger quantities of the stuff in hand—my contemporaries is considered
to be the literature in question. So confused now are we
between matter and treatment, between what is stated
and documented and what is prepared and presented,
that for the life of me I do not yet see whether we are
supposed to be building an ark or whether by immersion
and the meekest of submersions and an altogether complete submission of our distended and quite helpless car-
casses to its incalculable caprice we are supposed to be
celebrating and, in the whirling uncomfortable fashion of
flotsam at large, indicating and making visible the whole
tremendous cosmic inundation . . .[39]

The stuff of this discussion is Wells's response to James's
"Notes on Novelists"; the word "saturation" points
sufficiently to that. But the "treatment" is parodic only by
a little; "this fluid chaos that perpetually increases" is near
to James's "more or less juicy orange." And it is unfair to
Wells to read him as kinetic—falling off from serious
endeavor—while the Master worked in stasis. The exas-
peration registered here is not without cause. James, too,
had changed since their first meeting, and his prose could
prove as empty and ornate as the above. *The Golden Bowl*
offers many a paragraph by comparison with which Boon's
pastiche must be measured as restrained.

But Wells is more effective when he tackles James's
matter than when imitating the manner. They agreed that
a novel should represent and not deny "the sweet complexity of life, of the pointing this way and that . . ." Their
disagreement has to do with what should be represented,
and how. Here is Boon's central indictment. The mandarin's orange is small:

Then with the eviscerated people he has invented he begins to make up stories. What stories they are! Concentrated on suspicion, on a gift, on possessing a "piece" of old furniture, on what a little girl may or may not have noted in an emotional situation. These people cleared for artistic treatment never make lusty love, never go to angry war, never shout at an election or perspire at poker; never in any way *date*. . . . And upon the petty residuum of human interest left to them they focus minds of a Jamesian calibre . . .

The only living human motives left in the novels of Henry James are a certain avidity and an entirely superficial curiosity. Even when relations are irregular or when sins are hinted at, you feel that these are merely attitudes taken up, gambits before the game of attainment and over-perception begins . . . His people nose out suspicions, hint by hint, link by link. Have you ever known living human beings do that? The thing his novel is *about* is always there. It is like a church lit but without a congregation to distract you, with every light and line focused on the high altar. And on the altar, very reverently placed, intensely there, is a dead kitten, an eggshell, a bit of string . . . Like his "Altar of the Dead," with nothing to the dead at all . . . For if there was they couldn't be all candles and the effect would vanish. . . . And the elaborate, copious emptiness of the whole Henry James exploit is only redeemed and made endurable by the elaborate, copious wit. Upon the desert his selection has made Henry James erects palatial metaphors . . . The chief fun, the only exercise, in reading Henry James is this clambering over vast metaphors . . .[40]

Boon then proceeds to the image of the hippopotamus and the pea, which is the first example drawn from that text in this chapter. "It is," he claims, "leviathan retrieving pebbles." There follows a lengthy sketch of a novel "rather in the manner of Henry James" and "to be called 'The

Spoils of Mr. Blandish.'" Mr. Blandish hunts a house,
covets it, gets it, and studies the spirit of place. That spirit
is spirits ("1813 brandy, in considerable quantities bricked
up in a disused cellar of Samphire House"), and Mr. Blandish determines to sell. There are problems. The imagination staggers and the characters weave:

> You are never told the thing exactly. It is by indefinable
> suggestions, by exquisite approaches and startings back,
> by circumlocution the most delicate, that your mind at
> last shapes its realization that—the last drop of the last
> barrel has gone and that Mutimer, the butler, lies dead or
> at least helpless—in the inner cellar. And a beautiful
> flavour, ripe and yet rare, rich without opulence, hangs—
> *diminuendo morendo*—in the air . . .[41]

Some of this evokes James's acquisition of Lamb House
and his circumspect deciding. *The Spoils of Poynton* and
"The Turn of the Screw" return, it seems, to haunt their
author. Boon's version of James's advance upon scones
recalls James's note to Cora Crane when he confessed to a
passion for doughnuts. The pastiche is, intermittently,
acute. Here Mr. Blandish enters into possession of Samphire House:

> It was incredible. They were giving him tea with hot,
> inadvisable scones—but their hotness, their close heavi-
> ness, he accepted with a ready devotion, would have
> accepted had they been ten times as hot and close and
> heavy, not heedlessly, indeed, but gratefully, willingly
> paying his price for these astonishing revelations that
> without an effort, serenely, calmly, dropped in between
> her gentle demands whether he would have milk and her
> mild inquiries as to the exact quantity of sugar his habits
> and hygienic outlook demanded, that his hostess so cas-
> ually made. These generous, heedless people were talk-
> ing of departures, of abandonments, of, so they put it,
> selling the dear old place, if indeed any one could be

found to buy a place so old and so remote and—she
pointed her intention with a laugh—so very, very dear.
Repletion of scones were a small price to pay for such a
glowing, such an incredible gift of opportunity, thrust
thus straight into the willing, amazed hands . . .[42]

Wells delivered *Boon* to the Reform Club. One has to
wonder why. James was not there to receive it, but the
gesture is instructive: Wells had either the insouciance or
the obtuseness to think that his friend might not mind. He
had made a habit of the presentation copy and saw,
apparently, no reason to break with that pattern. It may
have been a further challenge or an instance of frank
ambivalence—as if Wells were saying, Let me face you
with the gauntlet, let it not come secondhand.

I have followed this last principle and let Boon speak
for himself. His representation of "the mind of the race"
scarcely urges "the peaceable kingdom," but James had
been attacked before and would be again. If it were not
for his response, the stimulus would be forgotten: *Boon* is
out of print. The dying James was roused to anger and to
produce a testament—two letters. His first response is
splendid. He writes on July 6, 1915. He mentions neither
the audacity nor the gracelessness of Wells's behavior; he
inclines the other cheek. Acknowledging receipt of the
book, he says he could not read it all, but:

> . . . I have more or less mastered your appreciation of
> H.J., which I have found very curious and interesting,
> after a fashion—though it has naturally not filled me with
> a fond elation. It is difficult of course for a writer to put
> himself *fully* in the place of another writer who finds him
> extraordinarily futile and void, and who is moved to pub-
> lish that to the world—and I think the case isn't easier
> when he happens to have enjoyed the other writer enor-
> mously, from far back; because there has then grown up
> the habit of taking some common meeting-ground

between them for granted, and the falling away of this is like the collapse of a bridge which made communication possible. But I am by nature more in dread of any fool's paradise, or at least of any bad misguidedness, than in love with the idea of a security proved, and the fact that a mind as brilliant as yours *can* resolve me into such an unmitigated mistake, can't enjoy me in anything like the degree in which I like to think I may be enjoyed, makes me greatly want to fix myself, for as long as my nerves will stand it, with such a pair of eyes. I am aware of certain things I have, and not less conscious, I believe, of various others that I am simply reduced to wish I did or could have; so I try, for possible light, to enter into the feelings of a critic for whom the deficiencies so preponderate. The difficulty about that effort, however, is that one can't keep it up—one *has* to fall back on one's sense of one's good parts—one's own sense; and I at least should have to do that, I think, even if your picture were painted with a more searching brush. For I should otherwise seem to forget what it is that my poetic and my appeal to experience rest upon. They rest upon *my* measure of fulness—fulness of life and of the projection of it, which seems to you such an emptiness of both . . .[43]

He then affirms once more "that interest may be, *must* be, exquisitely made and created . . ."; he excuses himself from lengthy explanation by suggesting that *Boon*'s chapter does not deserve it. He signs himself "Faithfully yours."

Wells answered immediately. On July 8, 1915, and beginning as always with "My Dear James," he continues:

You write me so kind and frank a letter after my offences that I find it an immense embarrassment to reply to you. I have set before myself a gamin-esque ideal, I have a natural horror of dignity, finish and perfection, a horror a little enhanced by theory. You may take it that my sparring and punching at you is very much due to the feeling that you were "coming over" me, and that if I was not very careful I should find myself giving way altogether to respect. There is of course a real and very fundamental difference in our innate and developed attitudes towards life and literature. To you literature like painting is an end, to me literature like architecture is a means, it has a use. . . .[44]

He then asserts, as we have seen, that the material for *Boon* was rescued from the wastepaper basket. He makes the central distinction, "I had rather be called a journalist than an artist." He apologizes and concludes: ". . . believe me, my dear James, your very keenly appreciative reader, your warm if rebellious and resentful admirer, and for countless causes yours most gratefully and affectionately/ H. G. Wells."

James's first letter began with the statement that "*Boon* . . . appears to have lurked . . . for a considerable time undelivered." It is difficult to know if he was telling the truth. That he wrote to Wells hard on the heels of his reading is, I think, demonstrable; he says he read it "yesterday" and would not have lied. Yet he may have collected the presentation copy Wells left at the Reform Club days or weeks before he opened it. And probably James knew by hearsay what he would find upon opening; he certainly knew it contained "your appreciation of H. J." Some kind or malicious third party would have told him what all London knew—he had been assaulted and had better be prepared. News travels fast when bad.

So there had been an anxious period of waiting, for Wells, between *Boon*'s delivery and James's response; the delay had tested him. His reaction feels effusive. He is nearly garrulous in his relief at receiving an answer, even though the answer had been chill. It is again a case of eating cake and hoping to have it thereafter—as if the public and the private man could be easily at odds. He hopes to explain himself further, but James is having none of it. He dictates a reply. This, too, arrives by return mail; it is dated July 10. He rejects both "the bad manners of *Boon*" and the excuse of the "waste-basket"; he holds the distinction between painting and architecture "for wholly null and void." His own views are not, he says, ascendant, not "coming over" Wells since nobody buys his books. He then takes Wells more particularly to task:

> But I *have* no view of life and literature, I maintain, other than that our form of the latter in especial is admirable exactly by its range and variety, its plasticity and liberality, its fairly living on the sincere and shifting experience of the individual practitioner. That is why I have always admired your so free and strong application of it, the particular rich receptacle of intelligences and impressions emptied out with an energy of its own, that your genius constitutes; and *that* is in particular why, in my letter of two or three days since, I pronounced it curious and interesting that you should find the case I constitute myself only ridiculous and vacuous to the extent of your having to proclaim your sense of it.[45]

The very fact of their association should be notable. Perhaps the small size of the literary community, or the assumption—still somehow current in England—that everyone knows everyone, was operative here. But the reader need only imagine a contemporary analogue to appreciate how strange a pairing off was James and Wells. (And time is a great leveler; it is like James's "agent who has bought up the lot of the most eligible to retail for a great procession." Those who purchase the wrong seats miss out on the parade. So what seems salient now may well have seemed obscure or indistinguishable then . . .)

Success seeks its own level, and like attracts like. We may make occasional forays across the literary tracks; we

may know each other glancingly or well. And there will be
exceptions to each rule. Yet the contemporary journalist
—by comparison, at least—has little serious commerce
with the contemporary mandarin. Wells had it in abundance:

> All this talk that I had with Conrad and Hueffer and
> James about the just word, the perfect expression, about
> this or that being "written" or not written, bothered me,
> set me interrogating myself, threw me into a heart-
> searching defensive attitude. I will not pretend that I got
> it clear all at once, that I was not deflected by their criti-
> cisms and that I did not fluctuate and make attempts to
> come up to their unsystematized, mysterious and elusive
> standards. But in the end I revolted altogether and
> refused to play their game. "I am a journalist," I
> declared, "I refuse to play the 'artist.' If sometimes I am
> an artist it is a freak of the gods. I am journalist all the
> time and what I write *goes now*—and will presently
> die."[40]

Modern as his attitudes appear, and prophetic as his
hopes and warnings proved, this perky assertion is true.
What he wrote *goes now* and is gone. His complaint that
James's characters "never in any way *date*" no longer
registers as forcible complaint. Even *Tono-Bungay*, his self-
confessed sustained attempt at meeting their "unsystema-
tized, mysterious and elusive standards," seems a period
piece. The rebirth of interest in Wells has more to do, I
think, with the fascinating figure he cut and his unassaila-
ble position as a father of "new journalism" than with his
books as such.

If the novel is continually dying, however, it is also and
continually being reborn. The genre has shape-shifted
before and will again. It is a confusing convenience of language that names Jane Austen's *Pride and Prejudice* and
William Burroughs's *The Ticket That Exploded*—to pick

two at random—both novels. They contain approximately the same number of words; they do not rhyme; and there all resemblances end. Even when, as in the words of Gordon Ray, "H. G. Wells tries to be a novelist," his work resembles that of James not much more closely than Burroughs's does Austen's.

The reverse is also the case. James's journalism is scarcely akin to that of Wells. Their two travel books on America make notable companion texts; it is as if they traverse two very separate continents that happen to have the same name. The eye of the beholder alters the thing seen. Had they in fact collaborated, the dialectic would have been compelling—but they remain a thesis and antithesis, at odds.

Such multiplicity within one genre is the contemporary rule. What seems exceptional here is that Wells and James were close—not that they disagreed. For as Aristotle observed, we only note the differences in those things that are essentially similar. They must share a category. Thus we would compare a horse and cow but not a horse and house. If we do the latter, we are being modernists, shifting categories. "Horse and house" have an orthographic and a sonorous relation, not one of sense—and the conjunction of these two posits a disjunction. They are separate if equal entities.

What complicates all this is the impulse to conjoin. James did offer to collaborate; Wells's youthful respect was sincere. A horse-house may seem "stable," but the relation is forced. We are told in grade school to contrast apples with oranges, and we contrast to compare. Yet both these authors sought converts. James was, if not proselytizing, at least so convinced an exemplar of his attitude to art that he must have seemed exemplary. Implicit in his pronouncements was the belief that aesthetic standards ought to be the rule. Without precisely coveting disciples, he was nonetheless a priest. He acquired acolytes. Part of his attraction toward the youthful and vivacious Crane and Wells no doubt entailed the attractive possibility of revision. He could make them over by taking them under his wing. When at Sandgate, Wells was tempted to follow James's lead; only later would he revolt. And *he* was consciously engaged in preachment; he spent much of his writing life as an apologist.

With better grace, and giving less offense, Wells repeated himself to James Joyce. In 1928 Joyce asked Wells for help with what would become *Finnegans Wake*. He hoped for public support from the eminent crusader and received instead a discourse as to eminent domain. They did not know each other well; there are no old scores to settle. Yet this letter carves out much the same position Wells had taken earlier, with James:

Lou Pidou, Saint Mathieu,
Grasse, A.M.
Nov. 23, 1928

My dear Joyce,

I've been studying you and thinking over you a lot. The outcome is that I don't think I can do anything for the propaganda of your work. I've an enormous respect for your genius dating from your earliest books and I feel now a great personal liking for you but you and I are set upon absolutely different courses. Your training has been Catholic, Irish, insurrectionary; mine, such as it was, was scientific, constructive and, I suppose, English. The frame of my mind is a world wherein a big, unifying and concentrating process is possible (increase of power and range by economy and concentration of effort), a *progress* not inevitable but interesting and possible. That game attracts and holds me. For it, I want language and statement as simple and clear as possible. . . .

Now with regard to this literary experiment of yours. It's a considerable thing because you are a very considerable man and you have in your crowded composition a mighty genius for expression which has escaped discipline. But I don't think it gets anywhere. You have turned your back on common men, on their elementary needs and their restricted time and intelligence and you have elaborated. What is the result? Vast riddles. Your last two works have been more amusing and exciting to write than they will ever be to read. Take me as a typical common reader. Do I get much pleasure from this work? No. Do I feel I am getting something new and illuminating as I do when I read Anrep's dreadful translation of Pavlov's badly written book on Conditioned Reflexes? No. So I ask: Who the hell is this Joyce who demands so many waking hours of the few thousands I have still to live for a proper appreciation of his quirks and fancies and flashes of rendering?

All this from my point of view. Perhaps you are right and I am all wrong. Your work is an extraordinary experiment and I would go out of my way to save it from destructive or restrictive interruption. It has its believers and its following. Let them rejoice in it. To me it is a dead end.

My warmest good wishes to you Joyce. I cant follow your banner any more than you can follow mine. But the world is wide and there is room for both of us to be wrong.

Yours,
H. G. Wells[47]

Conrad used a ship's crew as a model for society; it offered solidarity and an ordered, hierarchical ranking. James and Wells, as we have seen, used "boat" as a code word for work; images of shipwreck, leakage, and harbor abound. One synonym that binds the two words ("boat" and "work") is "craft." But craft itself is various; the clipper ship and speedboat must chart opposing courses, with a different crew and draw. The Cinque Ports have berthed both.

James died in 1916. He became a British subject; Wells attempted to become a Citizen of the World. Wells rehearsed their argument; James did not. Wells survived his elder colleague by fully thirty years; James had the last word. "It is art that *makes* life," he wrote, "makes interest, makes importance . . . and I know of no substitute whatever for the force and beauty of its process."[48] Their quarrel provides us with that.

V.
Group Portrait

The best things come, as a general thing, from the talents that are members of a group; every man works better when he has companions working in the same line, and yielding the stimulus of suggestion, comparison, emulation. Great things of course have been done by solitary workers; but they have usually been done with double the pains they would have cost if they had been produced in more genial circumstances. The solitary worker loses the profit of example and discussion; he is apt to make awkward experiments; he is in the nature of the case more or less of an empiric. The empiric may, as I say, be treated by the world as an expert; but the draw-

*backs and discomforts of empiricism re-
main to him, and are in fact increased by
the suspicion that is mingled with his gratitude, of a want in the public taste of a
sense of the proportion of things.*

—HENRY JAMES, Hawthorne, 1879

V.
Group Portrait

I write this in a garden half a day's journey by foot from any of the houses these authors once called home. A traveler in something slightly more efficient than Edith Wharton's motorcar can visit all their residences in one afternoon. The countryside is small-scale and the villages discrete. The lanes have been paved and the farmland increased. Kipling harnessed the Old Mill behind his home. With the help of a friend (who had organized the more substantial waters of the Nile at Aswan), he bought a deep-sea cable, dug a trench, and lit his lamps. This mill seems representative. First registered in the Domesday Book, it used to grind flour for farmers—and does so now again at an excessive price for visitors.

Tractors have transformed the Downs; oasthouses make elegant homes. Telephone and power poles complicate skyscapes with wires. The "County Fayre" is either self-consciously archaic or complete with stock-car racing and an electronic rifle range. Portable radios blare. When blacksmiths or sheepshearers ply their trade, it has the feel of wilful contrariety if they forego power tools; the smugglers in this region now arrive aboard the Hovercraft.

But the Weald of Kent has changed, I'd guess, less than many places in the British Isles and kept to its last more than most. James would recognize East Sussex and Rye— chock-full with tourists though it be—far more readily than London. As recently as 1377, Rye was laid waste by invaders: French knights who set it to the torch. The church bells stolen by the French were recovered the next year. Now the "Antient Town" invites such invasion and offers up its loot. And the balance of payments continues favorable. This is a prosperous corner of England, near enough to London for the weekend visitor and home to those executives who can arrive late at work. Hastings is a tourist center, as is Dover. The bodies sprawled on Camber Sands have not been washed ashore. They paint themselves with suntan oil, not woad. And even at their busiest the Cinque Ports feel sleepy, slightly; they have neither the bustle of Brighton nor the hum of Tunbridge Wells.

The advantages are many here and the problems few. Add climate to the relative economy of life outside the capital; add silence to the possibility of engaging speech. Add beauty to proximity of both the Continent and London; give a prospect of the sea. Have a populace polite to strangers, used to them, yet not overinclined to meddle. Claim an eminent author or two to provide cachet. Sustain a tradition of "artists-in-residence," from John Fletcher born in Rye to Thackeray who wrote of Winchelsea. (Sir Philip Sidney made his home in Kent, and Chaucer put her on the map immortally. Dickens and Shakespeare knew her well; Caesar deemed her the civilest place in all this isle.) These are the ingredients of such a stew as makes a colony.

Kipling lived in isolation; he cannot be called a member of the group. But he celebrates its landscape in "A Three-Part Song" from *Puck of Pook's Hill*:

I'm just in love with all these three,
The Weald an' the Marsh an' the Down countrie;
Nor I don't know which I love the most,
The Weald or the Marsh or the white chalk coast!

I've buried my heart in a ferny hill,
Twix' a liddle low shaw an' a great high gill.
Oh, hop-bine yaller an' wood-smoke blue,
I reckon you'll keep her middling true!

I've loosed my mind for to out an' run
On a Marsh that was old when Kings begun:
Oh, Romney level an' Brenzett reeds,
I reckon you know what my mind needs!

I've given my soul to the Southdown grass,
An' sheep-bells tinkled where you pass.
Oh, Firle an' Ditchling an' sails at sea,
I reckon you keep my soul for me![1]

Edward Ashburnham, Ford's "good soldier," has an honored Kentish name. Jack Kemp is the protagonist of Conrad and Ford's *Romance*; an actual John Kemp was the Archbishop of Canterbury. Young Etchingham Granger of *The Inheritors* inherited his first name from the nearby town of Etchingham. And for this present visitor, the region teems with ghosts. The spirits are not far removed; they have eyewitnesses. An elderly lady in Rye will recollect having heard James in the garden, dictating. His voice boomed, she says. Another will remember having been invited in, and how frightened of spilling the tea things she felt. Her husband recalls having met Conrad at the hairdresser's in Canterbury; he looked like an old oak tree, and he was very polite. "I remember," says this gentleman, "how gentlemanly Conrad was, how fine his boots were, and how he put me at my ease. I hadn't read a word of his, of course . . ." A relative of Moreton Frewen, Crane's landlord, sighs and says, "You know, they called him 'Mortal Ruin' in the city. For good reason, I'm afraid." And everywhere there's someone who knows someone who knew Wells.

The houses here retain the character of those who lived within. They reek of their old occupants. In some cases this is purposive: Bateman's has been preserved by the National Trust as Rudyard Kipling fashioned it. His writing desk, his inkwell, and his bric-a-brac remain in the study untouched. Lamb House, too, belongs to the National Trust. The house has been continually occupied —by such literary folk as E. F. Benson, Rumer Godden, and H. Montgomery Hyde. The garden pavilion where James wrote in summer was destroyed by the Second World War, and his papers have been dispersed. Yet the reception hall and telephone room retain the formal feel that visitors ascribed to the place when James was resident. An excellent example of early Georgian architecture (as Bateman's is of Jacobean), Lamb House once hosted the King. The Lamb family was powerful in Rye and figures in its history; their home stands at the top of a high, cobbled hill. But it does not soar in splendid isolation; it squeezes, rather, between the Mermaid Tavern and the church. Like its most famous tenant, it is nothing if not urbane.

Pent Farm is a very different matter. The cottage that Ford owned and Conrad inhabited still functions as a farm. It has been adapted to the owner's present needs. It is farther from the madding crowd than many might find comfortable, and unpretentious past the point of modesty. (Ford was a tall man; the ceilings are low; Jessie Conrad wrote with irritation that he used to thump for emphasis

on the ceiling above him which served as her floor.)
Conrad was proud of his view; he wrote in glowing terms
of the vista out his workroom window. This has been
blocked off by barns. No signpost points the way. And
when Conrad could afford to, he moved out. Yet the
hamlet of Postling cannot have changed much, nor the
feel of the Downs with a dark wood behind; the Pent
seems a ship beached alone.

Ford settled, turn by turn, in Bonnington, Limpsfield,
Postling, Aldington, and Winchelsea. Of his stay in the
region, he writes:

> . . . it is an infectious and holding neighborhood. Once
> you go there, you are apt there to stay. Or you will see in
> memory, the old walled towns, the red roofs, the grey
> stones, the country sweeping back in steps from the
> Channel to the North Downs, the great stretch of the
> Romney Marsh running out to Dungeness. In the Middle
> Ages they used to say: "These be the four quarters of the
> world: Europe, Asia, Africa and the Romney Marsh."
> But that was before Columbus committed his indis-
> cretion . . .[2]

"White Walls" at the top of Aldington Hill has the
cachet of rumor: smugglers are said to have hidden in its
cellar. But motion is Ford's hallmark, not an address. It
would be inappropriate to locate him exactly; he gives the
impression of a man at ease in other people's lodgings, in
hotels, or on the road. His roof was preferably old, his fur-
nishings distinguished; he wanted objects redolent of good
company and taste. Now "White Walls" has been gussied
up. Protective planting keeps it from the wind; the walls
are treated with high-gloss latex paint, not whitewash;
and the "veggies" back behind the garage have been rab-
bit-proofed. But Ford would not, I think, have minded; he
thought of himself as a transient and one who traveled
light.

Wells had many houses also; he is rootless, a time traveler. For the years of his proximity to and participation in this group, he was building his first home. Tubercular, he had been sent to the coast for reasons of health; he recovered rapidly. The building of Spade House—as he recalls in his autobiography—was a saving proposition for him and his wife, Jane. Characteristically, too, he started from scratch; he did not buy a previous structure and proceed to renovate. C. A. Voysey, an experimental architect, provided him with concepts then coming into vogue. The house had central heating, for instance, and its design anticipated the dictum that form follows function; it was well-appointed and placed. Very much a structure for the future, it nonetheless has failed to "weather" as impressively as Lamb House or Bateman's; it seems a period piece.

Brede Place has been burned. This is the oldest house of all, and the most capacious. A fourteenth-century manor, it passed into the Frewen family in the sixteenth century. It only recently was sold and will be rebuilt. For even its charred remnant has grandeur; the great walls and beams and gutted kitchen have the feel of that grim beauty enchanting to Crane. Not a place to spend the winter—not as sensible as Spade House for a sickly man. With its ancient chapel, massive shell, its fame as a smuggler's haven and gathering place for local ghosts, Brede is the stuff of romance. (Pretension, too, perhaps; it's the sort of stone pile that could sink a millionaire.) Crane was a bird of passage; he alighted briefly and then died. But it takes small imagination to provide the wrecked hulk in the hollow with an additional ghost. Sir Goddard Oxenbridge has company when the wind blows north northeast.

Ford chatted with the rural poor; Wells described the urban and suburban lower middle class. Edwardian Society was propped up at its wealthy best by people with slim chance of doing better, but the artist then as now had some real access to change. King Edward accepted Sir Thomas Lipton; why couldn't Wells's Mr. Polly or Edward Ponderevo dream of a welcome at court? Everywhere the sense of possibility seemed boundless; electricity and plumbing were within reach, if not grasp.

And though creature comforts seemed sometimes hard to come by, our authors have help. In 1901 of four million women in employment, one and a half million are in domestic service. In Hampstead there are eighty female domestics to every hundred occupants; in Westminster in addition there are twelve menservants. (By 1951 only one percent of British households—including hotels and institutions—would have any servants at all.) In the 1906 edition of *Mrs. Beeton's Book of Household Management*, the following "simple" summer breakfast is proposed:

> Wholewheat Porridge
> Ham Omelet
> Poached Eggs on Toast
> Fried Whiting
> Grilled Kidneys
> Potted Beef
> Galantine of Chicken
> Strawberries
> Scones, Rolls, Toast, Bread
> Butter, Marmalade, Jam
> Tea, Coffee, Cream, Milk.[3]

Then there is a spread at lunch. One hesitates to reproduce the menu for a feast; here Mr. Polly takes his modest meal:

> There had been the cold pork from Sunday, and some nice cold potatoes and Randall's Mixed Pickles, of which he was inordinately fond. He had eaten three gherkins, two onions, a small cauliflower head, and several capers

with every appearance of appetite, and indeed with avidity; and then there had been cold suet pudding to follow, with treacle, and then a nice bit of cheese. It was the pale, hard sort of cheese he liked; red cheese, he declared, was indigestible. He had also had three big slices of greyish baker's bread, and had drunk the best part of the jugful of beer . . .[4]

The collocation of foreigners then gathering in England would not as likely have gathered in any other country—or none in which the English language was a native tongue. And it must be remembered that Great Britain in 1900 construed itself as plausibly the most powerful nation on earth. It had none of the feel at any rate of a cultural backwater; Americans traveled to England in order to swim in the mainstream of art. With his fine phrase, "The London Yankees," Stanley Weintraub indicates how authors such as Twain and Harte—or painters like John Singer Sargent—could seek companionship and wealth in the British Isles. Henry James's exile—like that of the Americans in Paris later—was not so much a repudiation of his homeland as a hunt for something more. And that additional something was abundantly in England: a widespread acceptance of and interest in the arts.

Before things fell apart, moreover, there must have been a center that would hold. These writers' protagonists are rarely writers; they are men of the actual world. One signal of the way our age has increased in specialization is the self-reflexive novel; in theory as in practice, now, we tend to offer primacy to the world within the word. Surely the novelist's concern with form has increased in this century, and the "manner" of the "matter" is taking pride of place. Gide and Joyce have as much to do with this as James, but the generality applies: more books have been produced of late with the novelist as hero than ever before. Of what else may the writer write authoritatively;

what other way of working may he comprehend? Such
discretion in the arts is natural enough and may prove the
better part of valor—but it does keep things discrete.

A younger Edwardian, E. M. Forster, put it differently.
His epigraph for *Howards End* may be read as an injunction: "Only Connect." The severe scrutiny of standards
that proved James's abiding concern is predicated on the
assumption that there are such standards and that they
might abide. Ford's protagonists—most notably Christopher Tietjens in the great tetralogy—are powered by the
conservative's faith: that there's something to conserve.
And one of the things that literati will naturally wish to
preserve is simple literacy, the sense of the past in prose.
It was an ideal of the academy without walls, and all these
men were autodidacts to a marked degree. No single one
of them had what can be described as a conventional edu-
cation, but that they were educated is beyond dispute.
The role of Academe as grove and haven for the creative
writer did not then pertain. Nor were any of them—at
least as of 1900—welcome in Oxford and Cambridge. I
cannot escape the suspicion that these authors, had they
been provided with lectureships and chairs, would have
sought each other out the less. They were not quite
comme il faut—as Edmund Gosse and the arbiters of literary London would have it—and we should be grateful.
The innovative artist is an outlaw even when he wears a
three-piece suit. One makes one's calls by telephone now,
and letter-writing is in consequence extinct; instant access
to reviews can obviate the time-consuming need to read
a book.

In the context of the library, colleagueship extends to
those one has not met—to the writers one admires.
Friendship sometimes intervenes; it causes one to make
more of one's own associates than sheer objective assess-

ment would have it. Personal distaste can have an equal and opposite effect. Therefore, it is easier in ways to think of one's colleagues as distant or dead, to fashion a community of writers *in absentia*. The truth is that most of one's masters are dead or distant anyway: Homer and Dante and Dickens are unavailable for drinks. We all are apprenticed to a fast-vanishing guild, and time has little to do with membership therein. The dancer cannot pattern his work closely on Nijinsky's, nor can the cellist on Boccherini's—since those legendary performers are but the stuff of legend once their performance is done. They antedate the apparatus of retention: tape and film. But Cervantes's words remain, as do those of Lawrence Sterne or Lady Murasaki, and the purposively random nature of this list should prove just how present those past masters are.

Every writer, in short, works with a double standard. The first is comparative. This applies both to the self's previous achievement and to the achievement of more or less celebrated contemporaries. It's the sort of disease that a writer calls health to think each word he has written is rotten and every word to come will prove superb. He wants to write a masterpiece and is haunted by suspicions that his work is mediocre; he wants to earn his colleagues' admiration and garners scorn, indifference, or envy. He wants the world's attention but on his own terms only, wanting also to be left alone. There's always this notion of plausible growth and the consequent fear of decline: a career exists in flux.

Take the example of Conrad. When old and rich and honored, he produced little of note. In a not uncommon irony attached to the profession, he lived to see his manuscripts resold for vastly more than he had received when writing them in need. John Quinn, the book collector, "had invested about $10,000 in Conrad and was returned a thousand percent profit."[5] In the auction of the Quinn collection, Conrad's work proved far the most valuable: the manuscript of *Victory* fetched four times as much as Joyce's *Ulysses*. That which compels expression may then cause the pen to run dry.

This is the trope or paradox that Conrad confronted at length. Though laurel-covered in his sixties, he took small consolation in the laurels. He spent as much time grappling with the pages of *The Rescue* as with his earlier career at sea; to complete the one, perhaps, was to extinguish all vivid recollection of the other. Though faithful to the surface touches, he renounced the depths—becoming, in effect, the simple spinner of yarns for whom he had been earlier mistaken.

He knew this, apparently. He referred to himself as drowning, exhausted; the prickly exactness of his behavior when old carries with it somewhere a whiff of self-reproof. Conrad squabbled with his family and friends, aware he'd been outmoded but uncertain if his place of honored relegation to the lists of "past masters" was modish or would last. He refused a proffered knighthood, in part because of doubt as to his own authentic Englishness; the Nobel Prize he coveted, however, was awarded in the year of his death to another Polish author, Wladislaw Reymont.

Yet it is in the context of some such term as "fidelity" that Conrad's greatness resides. His work exalts unswerving loyalty, an elected single-mindedness. (Those who are single-minded without conscious choice verge on the comical, as with Captain MacWhirr of "Typhoon.") His heroes' ideals may vary. They may commit themselves to various versions of that bubble, reputation—but they share with their creator the steadfast resolution that a task once set should be seen through. Perhaps no other artist so entirely expresses that sense of embattled commitment we now name existential; few have proved so competent to turn their special previous competency into the stuff of art. The sea was Conrad's alkahest, the leaden hours of the watch the time he would transform. And it provided him with just the realm of gold as experience that the self-reflexive novel by definition lacks. The alchemy is simple: it helps to have something to write. As Henry James assured him:

> No one has *known*—for intellectual use—the things you know, and you have, as the artist of the whole matter, an authority no one has approached. I find you in it all writing wonderfully, whatever you may say of your difficult medium and your *plume rebelle*. You knock about in the wide waters of expression like the raciest and boldest of privateers.[6]

Even the best-humored author has some degree of competitive anxiety; the king keeps only a few harpers in his hall. And there are places more near the fire, or choicer cuts of meat—our artists were not guiltless of jostling for position. Take the model of the court under some such canny and tight-fisted monarch as Queen Elizabeth I. She knew she could not keep her retinue of courtiers at a living wage; they were legion, and hungry. So she encouraged them to sing for supper and the say-so possibility of gain; if Walter Raleigh were vastly rewarded for flinging his cloak in a puddle, why couldn't Fortune crook her finger at some other someone next year? So season in and season out, the court bought a dream of riches and fame —a dream to be realized by few. It cost the Exchequer a good deal less to reward one single courtier out of all proportion than to reward all courtiers with their due and proper meed.

Such systems breed rage. They are the norm today. We work so hard for what turns out to be the taste of ashes in a toothless mouth. What we thought we were doing we fail to have done; if we succeed it's often as not accidental. We dream of influence; it's effluence instead. The average wage is a penny a page; the average reward is anonymity. If your name is well enough known to be taken, then it's likely to be so in vain, or mispelled; vanity and the deep paralysis of repetition await those who truly succeed. Those who hunt success too consciously are conscious of too little else; those to whom it comes unbidden do its bidding soon . . .

But the point I hope to make is that marketplace standards must be in essence comparative: "I'm doing better this year than last; I'm writing less well today than last Thursday; he's more famous than I am, or than he deserves." Yet the standards of the craft are absolute. This is not to say that such standards are immutable, or that they can be defined. I know of no such coherent statement and mistrust the very notion that it might exist. This book proposes none. The iterated assertion of faith soon enough becomes asseveration; tomorrow's *Blast* will prove yesterday's echo. That art is descriptive is clear, that art is prescriptive is to be desired, but that it is proscriptive seems to me inane. Dangerous, too, since that way lies repression. . . . The virtue of the marketplace lies in its uncensored jumble, its multiplicity of wares. And they must exist side by side. Few hierarchical systems are more of a muddle than aesthetics; how explain why *Moby Dick*'s a better book than *Jaws*?

Still, every writer worth his salt has some vision of perfection, some dream of the realized ideal. This is likely to be a compound of his own alerted reading—the models he has taken—his best intentions for his still-to-be-accomplished work, and aspiration too gossamer to name: a color that washes the visible world, a half-remembered snatch of song, the beauty in belief. The forms such aspiration takes are various, and must be, but this is where that double standard obtains. Because the apprentice writer aims for glory even more than fame, and glory is an absolute; we need no codified aesthetic to know where it resides.

All this should adumbrate another thesis of *Group Portrait*: it is less instructive to discuss the better than the best. I don't mean to say that our writers thought themselves or called each other immortal. Nor was Rye a self-conscious and self-styled retreat; Wells's description of the James cenacle is more than a little unkind. But these men gave themselves wholly over to art, and they represented to each other—as well as to the public—austere claims of the calling. James did act as a sort of arbiter, the legatee of George Eliot, Flaubert, and Turgenev. Ford assumed the role of artist as archeditor, and Conrad's pronouncements were priestly in tone and intent.

Therefore, it can be argued that the double standard cited above has double application. The group could read each other's work not only in the spirit of comparison but also as an emblem of the absolute. At any rate, they were each other's editorial consciences; after the gossip and the denigration waned, there remained respect. Conrad's preface to "The Nature of a Crime" is a weary piece of prose, denying the work's worth. But he closes it as follows:

> After signing these few prefatory words, I will pass the pen to him [Ford] in the hope that he may be moved to contradict me on every point of fact, impression and appreciation. I said "the hope." Yes. Eager hope. For it would be delightful to catch the echo of the desperate, earnest, eloquent and funny quarrels which enlivened those old days. The pity of it that there comes a time when all the fun of one's life must be looked for in the past![7]

That elegiac note (the preface was composed the year of Conrad's death) rings often in his reminiscences, as well as those of Ford. Garnett titled his memoir *The*

Golden Echo, and time does gild the daily dross; in retrospect the prewar years would seem untroubled, gay. This
is perhaps a roundabout way of stating a manifest truth:
it's nice to like the work of people you have liked. All
groups indeed must promulgate their own and special
excellence in order to perceive themselves as a group; it
helps if others recognize this also, and the achievement
is real.

The achievements were real. At the end of Victoria's
life, this century began; the innovators, renegades, and
prophets of that year are our ancestors. No author writing
in English today can fail to deal with Conrad and James;
no living writer is more powerful than in their heydays
were Kipling and Wells. The careers of Crane and Ford
are representative also of ways we function still; what
meteoric rise and fall is more so than was Stephen Crane's,
what example of staying power more poignant than Ford's?
It is a commonplace by now that the artist, doubly dis-
tanced, must imagine home. He makes of the landscape
what Gerard Manley Hopkins called "inscape" and fash-
ions for himself a fictive "new found land." In a literature
of alienation, the actual alien may well have an advantage.
These men were all to a degree exiles, with a romantic
feel for the properly organized place. For Ford this was
the "Great Trade Route," for Wells the anticipated utopia,
but the impulse is equivalent: a dream of worlds in order,
with the ordering aided by words.

I myself was born in England, of German-Jewish parents
and with an Italian name; I make my home in Vermont.
The notion of a chosen land, of momentary rootedness
and roots that are self-nurtured, has personal importance, clearly. The first word of this paragraph was "I,"
and "I" have appeared throughout. The personal pronoun
embarrasses me, but it feels appropriate; these notes will
have value when read as first-person report.

✿ ✿ ✿

The book is twenty-four magazines, really. It states that it is "To be completed in about 20 Fortnightly Parts," but Wells was always garrulous. *The Outline of History*, "being a plain history of Life and Mankind," begins in Part I with "The Making of Our World" and ends with "The Next Stage." The cover illustration of Part I shows a cave man sitting on a boulder and staring at a sunset. His body, thickly muscled, is midnight blue and black; the rocks behind him are yellow and red. His pose is somehow similar to that of Rodin's "The Thinker," but we do not know what he is thinking or what he sees out there off the magazine's edge.

Part 24 has a map on its cover. Its colors are soft blue and green and ocher; it bears the inspiriting legend "The United States of the World." After "The International Catastrophe of 1914," the final installment proposes "The Possible Unification of the World Into One Community of Knowledge and Will." The magazines are bound in cloth-jointed casing; the slipcase is blue leather and its title is gold leaf.

My parents acquired this object; I have it still. What cheerful, sprightly faith it represents! how fittingly the advertisements for piano and language instruction dovetail with the downfall of the Assyrian Empire. The inside sheet of Part 15 ("Crusader, Turk and Mongol") advertises Drummer Dyes, Laitova Lemon Cheese ("the daily spread for the children's bread"), Rexine ("the ideal furniture covering"), and Mackintosh Toffee Deluxe. I have but to slip the sections from their slipcase and out comes my elder brother, with his magic gift of literacy, his "Can't you see I'm busy?" while he bends to the page. Later, when he put off childish things, he handed me this comic-bookish, skewed, and wondrous text.

We all invent our pasts. I cannot remember the moment

when I began to speak and cannot remember the moment
at which I decided to write. Rather, and naturally, the
whole is a continuum. It is a series of moments and set of
lines crossed that appear far clearer in retrospect than
they ever did in prospect. To take one such example, I
remember learning how to read. I had just turned six years
old and was with my family on the S.S. *Queen Elizabeth*,
crossing from Southampton to New York. On the third day
of the voyage out—having passed some watermark that
meant we were closer to America—I received my first pair
of long pants. And that afternoon (sitting cross-legged on
the stateroom floor, so proud of my flannels I hated to
crease them, the sun through the porthole spotlighting the
letters) I taught myself to read. It was a book about boats.
There was a lighthouse, a bridge, a series of ships—from
trireme to frigate, canoe to destroyer, with two whole
pages devoted to the fireboats, their spray a white, wet
arc.

The captions distinguished between them; so could I.
The alphabet's tumblers went "click." I remember the feel
of it, the pride in it, the pleasure, the way the world made
sense. I think I remember telling my father I had no time
for shuffleboard; I know I took the book up to the deck for
tea. It was wonderful: the way the lines pictured this life I
was leading. Everything signified; everything fit. Our
steward was called Jonathan; I recognized his badge as
his name. The rest of the trip is a jumble, but this sudden
perception of order—the deck chairs ranked in rows like
language, how a page is organized and why you turn it
when—remains indelible. I learned to read that day.

Three years ago, however, I was sorting through some
papers in the attic of my father's house. He was moving
once again, and I had come to help discard the past's
detritus. In a box full of grade-school report cards, letters
home from camp, and other such accumulation, I came

across a book titled *Henry's Green Wagon*. It was familiar,
faintly; it conjured up Great Britain, not the United
States. The boy on the disintegrating cover was pink-
cheeked and wearing blue shorts. I read the inscription.
"To Master Nicky Delbanco," it said. "The best reader in
Miss Jamaica's Kindergarten Class. Congratulations. First
Prize."

Miss Jamaica's was the school across the street. Like any
English child, I had been taught to read *before* the age of
six. So the memory is false. It is clear but confused.
Although I remember the school, the vast-seeming
meadow I would traverse on the way home, the hedge-
hog's lair, the way my aunt would shepherd us, a clearing
in the woods that I called Hansel's house—though I
remember much of this I had forgotten I knew how to
read. There are explanations. Probably I learned in stages.
Maybe I faked it with *Henry's Green Wagon*, having
memorized the book and turning the pages when it
seemed proper to turn. That sun-shot moment on the
Queen Elizabeth may have illuminated something else
instead. The transatlantic crossing was a rite of passage,
after all, and what I learned while sitting on the deck
chair may not have been the alphabet. Therefore, the critic's question: how accurate are such accounts?

Herewith, according to the British Library Association,
is an index of the increase in the reading public. In 1880
there had been 95 British library authorities; in 1900 there
were 352. The books in stock more than doubled from the
period of 1896 to 1911, and the books issued more than
doubled (from 26 to 54 million) also. But popularity was
not then—any more than it had been before or will be
again—an indication of lastingness; the "queens of the cir-
culating libraries" are not now household names. Ford en-
vied the "lady novelists" their success, but M. E. Braddon,

Mrs. Henry Wood, Emma Jane Worboise, Marie Corelli, Mrs. M. W. Hungerford, and Ouida have lost their currency. Nor have such men as Fergus Hume, Frank Barrett, E. Phillips Oppenheim, Guy Boothby, or William Le Queux endured. *A Century of Best Sellers 1830-1930* offers this list for the Edwardian period. Desmond Flower, who compiled and introduced the list, defines "best sellers" as works of fiction that "not only have reached six figures in a fairly short time, but which, during the long or the short life that fate allowed them, took the country by storm and, in many instances, affected the reading tastes of the British public":

1901   *Anna Lombard,* by Victoria Cross
        The History of Sir Richard Calmady, by Lucas Malet
1902   *The Four Feathers,* by A. E. W. Mason
1903   *When It Was Dark,* by Guy Thorne
1904   *Baccarat,* by Frank Danby
        The Garden of Allah, by Robert Hichens
1905   *The Boy in Green,* by Nat Gould
        The Morals of Marcus Ordeyne, by W. J. Locke
        The Scarlet Pimpernel, by Baroness Orczy
        The Four Just Men, by Edgar Wallace
1907   *Three Weeks,* by Elinor Glyn
1908   *The Blue Lagoon,* by H. de Vere Stacpoole
1909   *The Rosary,* by Florence Barclay
1910   *The Broad Highway,* by Jeffery Farnol[8]

Clearly, "the reading tastes of the British public" as of 1900 do not coincide with those of the critic eighty years later; such works as *Lord Jim* and *The Ambassadors* are not remotely near the top of the list. They earned then, and increasingly, the cognoscenti's admiration—but that was and is a mixed blessing. To the writer who writes for a living, the support of his peers is welcome indeed, but the reading public pays the bills. The letters of these artists have more to do with problems fiscal than artistic. They did not eat aesthetics or heat their homes with manuscript; they could not drink ink. The business of artistry is after all also a business, and profit mattered to Conrad or James quite as much as to their publishers. It may disconcert the reader who hunts lofty speculation to read how often writers speculate in the less than lofty realm of royalties and reprint and serial rights. The business letter is more likely to be preserved in the files than a purely personal note. So it's possible here also that we have a skewed perspective. But the plight of these authors has at least this single strain in common: writing yields a paltry wage, and one to be eked out.

Conrad wrote an article, "Henry James." A phrase thereof bears repeating:

> When the last aqueduct shall have crumbled to pieces, the last airship fallen to the ground, the last blade of grass have died upon a dying earth, man, indomitable by his training in resistance to misery and pain, shall set this undiminished light of his eyes against the feeble glow of the sun.[9]

William Faulkner may have read that sentence. His Nobel Prize acceptance speech, in 1950, sounds more than coincidentally echoic:

> It is easy enough to say that man is immortal simply because he will endure: that when the last ding-dong of doom has clanged and faded from the last worthless rock hanging tideless in the last red and dying evening, that even then there will be still one more sound; that of his puny inexhaustible voice, still talking. I refuse to accept this. I believe that man will not merely endure; he will prevail.[10]

Good writers borrow and great writers steal. What

Shakespeare did to Holinshed would nowadays put him in court. The whole notion of originality is modern and, to a degree, peculiar; it failed to interest those who composed *Gilgamesh* or *Beowulf.* So the authenticity of Faulkner's voice is not in question here. And though he met neither Conrad nor James, he may well have been influenced by both. It is not beyond the reach of ingenuity to suggest a grouping in these credos. One could even argue that the echo, if unconscious, is more deeply structured than would have been a paraphrase. The similarities here outstrip syntax. Since there's nothing new under "the feeble glow of the sun," the problem becomes one of restating "old verities and truths of the heart." The first phrase is Conrad's, the second Faulkner's, and they seem to me legitimately conjoined.

We each experience everything these authors described by the time we're five, if not before. We're familiar with gain, loss, love, hate, life, death, riches, poverty, laughter, sorrow, the very marrow of society. We grow by, among other things, growing in the gift of putting all this into words. The problem for the artist, then, is to find some sufficiently available innovative context for the old, old truths. And this takes time, takes a lot more than our first five years to learn—takes information in abundance, the relentless pack-rat accumulation of fact. All writers read all the time. They carry books like talismans and flatter each other by imitation. If the problem of influence and the possibilities of fruitful interchange continue, then there should be present examples. These novelists did not hesitate to offer their opinions; I have taken that as license to propose my own.

The reader will have noticed—as Ford was fond of remarking—that this final chapter is digressive. That is intentional: a record of impressions should advance by indirection. The issue all along has been not what to cite and note but what I might legitimately leave out. James gave Kipling's bride away; Ford's favorite device was the ellipse. . . .

The Polish word for paradise, for example, is pronounced "rye." Conrad would have found the coincidence pleasant and remarked upon it once or twice—perhaps even habitually—to his confreres in heaven. I have no doubt of this but cannot document it and have therefore (till this paragraph) left the pun alone. So, too, with much that's much more consequential: their politics, their sexual proclivities, their neuroses, poetry, siblings, and clothes. *Group Portrait* will have served its turn if a great deal remains still to say.

Whether one calls it a movement or group, whether one insists on influence or describes it as collegiality, whether the friendships were lasting or transient, this much is irreducible: five major talents worked in close proximity. And the contact was not accidental or occasioned by geography alone. If that is the most one can claim, it is nonetheless sufficient, and the burden of these chapters has been to claim rather more. Though writing is a solitary business, it need not be a hermit's; though authors hunt and court success, it need not come at each other's expense. I would instead urge the reverse. We all are richer for the writings of our great originals; why should we feel the poorer if greatness exists in our time?

On the face of it, these five are as different the one from the other as five practitioners of any single discipline could be. But they had in common ambition, a tolerance for variety, and a recognition of the stringent demands of craft. They aided each other, or tried to, and the aid and comfort helped. In that regard they were exemplary, and we can profit from the example. This is true for the reader as well as the writer: generous attention is its own reward.

I have attempted to avoid the stump speech, but it is implicit in *Group Portrait* and explicit in this chapter's epigraph: "The best things come, as a general thing, from the talents that are members of a group."

Notes

I. Figures in a Landscape

1. Ford Madox Ford, *The Bodley Head Ford Madox Ford*, Vol. V (London: The Bodley Head Ltd., 1971), pp. 278–279.

2. Stephen Crane, in Thomas Beer, *Stephen Crane* (New York: Alfred A. Knopf, 1923), p. 233.

3. John Galsworthy, Introduction, W. H. Hudson, *Green Mansions* (New York: Alfred A. Knopf, 1916), p. xi.

4. Stephen Crane, *The O'Ruddy, The Works of Stephen Crane*, Vol. IV (Charlottesville: University Press of Virginia, 1971), pp. 15–16.

5. Henry James, *The Letters of Henry James*, Vol. I, ed. Percy Lubbock (New York: Charles Scribner's Sons, 1920), pp. 310–312.

6. Joseph Conrad, Preface, *The Nigger of the "Narcissus"* (New York: Doubleday, Page & Co., 1924), p. 14.

7. Virginia Woolf, in Richard Ellman, *Golden Codgers* (New York: Oxford University Press, 1973), p. 113.

8. W. B. Yeats, Introduction, *Oxford Book of Modern Verse* (New York: Oxford University Press, 1936), pp. xi–xii.

9. Henry James to Mrs. Humphry Ward, in Stanley Weintraub, *The London Yankees* (New York: Harcourt Brace Jovanovich, Inc., 1979), p. 167.

10. Joseph Conrad, *A Personal Record* (New York: Doubleday, Page & Co., 1923), p. vii.

11. Joseph Conrad, *Heart of Darkness* (New York: Doubleday, Page & Co., 1921), p. 257.

12. H. G. Wells, *Experiment in Autobiography* (New York: The Macmillan Co., 1934), pp. 410–411.

13. Ada Galsworthy notebook, in Catherine Dupré, *John Galsworthy* (New York: Coward, McCann & Geoghegan, 1976), p. 135.

14. Frederick R. Karl, *Joseph Conrad, The Three Lives* (New York: Farrar, Straus & Giroux, 1979), p. 411.

II. Stephen Crane in England

The title of this chapter, and much of its argument, derives from Eric Solomon's *Stephen Crane in England: A Portrait of the Artist* (Columbus: Ohio State University Press, 1964).

1. Stephen Crane, "The Ghost," *The Works of Stephen Crane,* Vol. VIII (Charlottesville: University Press of Virginia, 1971), p. 163.

2. Ford Madox Ford, *Return to Yesterday* (New York: H. Liveright & Co., 1932), pp. 36–37.

3. H. G. Wells, *Experiment in Autobiography* (New York: The Macmillan Co., 1934), pp. 522–523.

4. Stephen Crane to Moreton Frewen, January 1, 1900, as cited in R. W. Stallman, *Stephen Crane* (New York, George Braziller, 1968), pp. 494–495.

5. Stephen Crane, "The Ghost," *The Works of Stephen Crane,* Vol. VIII, p. 170.

6. *The Manchester Guardian,* January 13, 1900.

7. *The Sussex Express, The Surrey Standard, The Kent Mail,* Friday, January 5, 1900.

8. A.E.W. Mason to Vincent Starrett, October 4, 1945, *Stephen Crane, Letters,* eds. R. W. Stallman and Lillian Gilkes (New York: New York University Press, 1960), p. 343.

9. Edith Ritchie Jones, "Stephen Crane At Brede," *The Atlantic Monthly,* July, 1954, p. 55.

10. Ford, *Return to Yesterday,* p. 35.

11. Wells, *Experiment in Autobiography,* p. 524.

12. Stephen Crane, in John Berryman, *Stephen Crane* (New York: William Sloane Associates, 1950), p. 248.

13. Willa Cather, "When I Knew Stephen Crane," from *The Library,* in *Stephen Crane,* ed. Maurice Bassan (Englewood Cliffs, N.J.: Prentice-Hall, 1967), p. 17.

14. Stephen Crane, "An Episode of War," *The Works of Stephen Crane,* Vol. VI, p. 90.

15. Crane, "The Veteran," ibid., p. 86.

16. Richard Harding Davis, *Harper's Magazine,* May, 1899.

17. Leon Edel, *Henry James,* Vol. V (Philadelphia: J. B. Lippincott Co., 1952), p. 65.

18. Stephen Crane, "The Squire's Madness," *The Works of Stephen Crane,* Vol. VIII, p. 196.

19. Lillian Gilkes, *Cora Crane* (Bloomington: Indiana University Press, 1960), p. 254.

20. Thomas Beer, *Stephen Crane* (New York: Alfred A. Knopf, 1923), pp. 169–170.

21. Ford, *Return to Yesterday,* pp. 38–39.

22. Beer, *Stephen Crane,* p. 170.

23. Ford, *Return to Yesterday,* p. 9.

24. Ford Madox Ford, Preface, *Joseph Conrad: A Personal Remembrance* (New York: Octagon Books, 1971), pp. vi–vii.

25. Eudora Welty, from a review of Arthur Mizener's *The Saddest Story: A Biography of Ford Madox Ford,* in Welty's *The Eye of the Storm* (New York: Random House, 1977), p. 250.

26. Stephen Crane to Thomas Hutchinson, 1899, *Stephen Crane, Letters,* eds. Stallman and Gilkes, pp. 250–251.

27. Henry James to Cora Crane, *The Letters of Henry James,* Vol. I, ed. Percy Lubbock (New York: Charles Scribner's Sons, 1920), p. 315.

28. Henry James to H. G. Wells, *Henry James and H. G. Wells,* eds. Leon Edel and Gordon H. Ray (Urbana: University of Illinois Press, 1955), p. 68.

29. Joseph Conrad, Introduction, Thomas Beer, *Stephen Crane,* p. 3.

30. Ibid., pp. 11–12.

31. Ibid., p. 17.

32. Ibid., p. 30.

33. Ibid., p. 33.

34. Stephen Crane, "Concerning the English Academy," *The Works of Stephen Crane*, Vol. VIII, p. 734.

35. Joseph Conrad, "Stephen Crane: A Note Without Dates, 1919," reprinted in *Notes on Life and Letters* (New York: Doubleday, Page & Co., 1924), p. 50.

36. Joseph Conrad to Stephen Crane, *Stephen Crane, Letters*, eds. Stallman and Gilkes, p. 154.

37. Edith Ritchie Jones, "Stephen Crane At Brede," *The Atlantic Monthly*, July, 1954, p. 57.

38. Joseph Conrad to Edward Garnett, *Letters From Joseph Conrad* (Indianapolis: Bobbs-Merrill Co., 1928), p. 118.

39. Joseph Conrad to an unknown recipient, ibid., pp. 321–322.

40. Conrad, "Stephen Crane: A Note Without Dates," pp. 51–52.

41. H. G. Wells to Stephen Crane, *Stephen Crane, Letters*, eds. Stallman and Gilkes, p. 276.

42. H. G. Wells, "Stephen Crane From an English Standpoint," *North American Review*, CLXXI (August 1900), p. 23.

43. Stephen Crane, *The O'Ruddy, The Works of Stephen Crane*, Vol. IV, p. xxxi.

44. Ibid., p. 37.

45. Ibid., p. 34.

46. Robert Barr to Karl Harriman, *Stephen Crane, Letters*, eds. Stallman and Gilkes, p. 287.

47. Quoted by Moreton Frewen to Cora Crane, June 16, 1900, *The O'Ruddy, The Works of Stephen Crane*, Vol. IV, p. xlix.

48. Cora Crane to Pinker, *Stephen Crane, Letters*, eds. Stallman and Gilkes, pp. 267–268.

49. Robert Barr to Willis Clarke, quoted by Thomas Beer in the introduction to *The O'Ruddy, Work of Stephen Crane*, ed. Wilson Follett (New York: Alfred A. Knopf, 1925), Vol. VII, pp. x–xi.

50. Stephen Crane, quoted by Cora Crane in "For Use in Stephen's Life," *The Works of Stephen Crane*, Vol. IV, p. xxiii.

51. Stephen Crane, in Thomas Beer, *Stephen Crane*, p. 231.

52. Stephen Crane, "Howells Fears the Realists Must Wait," *The Works of Stephen Crane*, Vol. VIII, p. 638.

53. Cyril Connolly, *Enemies of Promise* (Boston: Little, Brown & Co., 1939), p. 131.

54. Joseph Conrad to Edward Garnett, *Letters From Joseph Conrad*, p. 155.

55. H. G. Wells, "Stephen Crane From an English Standpoint," *North American Review*, p. 24.

56. Stephen Crane, "Stephen Crane Says: Edwin Markham Is His First Choice For The American Academy," *The Works of Stephen Crane*, Vol. VIII, p. 758.

57. Stephen Crane, "Ouida's Masterpiece," ibid., Vol. VIII, p. 677.

58. Stephen Crane, "War Is Kind," ibid., Vol. X, p. 54.

III. Conrad and Ford

1. Joseph Conrad, *A Personal Record* (New York: Doubleday, Page & Co., 1923), p. 205.

2. Ibid., p. 250.

3. Ford Madox Ford, *Joseph Conrad: A Personal Remembrance* (New York: Octagon Books, 1971), p. 3.

4. Ibid., pp. 7–8.

5. H. G. Wells, *Experiment in Autobiography* (New York: The Macmillan Co., 1934), pp. 526–527.

6. Joseph Conrad to H. G. Wells, October 20, 1905, in Gerard Jean-Aubry, *Joseph Conrad: Life and Letters*, Vol. II (Garden City, N.Y.: Doubleday, 1927), p. 25.

7. J. H. Morey, *Joseph Conrad and Ford Madox Ford: A Study in Collaboration*, unpublished dissertation, Cornell University, 1960. This is a complete and judicious account of the collaboration; it should be made available to the general reading public.

8. Ford, *Joseph Conrad: A Personal Remembrance*, pp. 92–93.

9. Ibid., p. 94

10. Simon Pure, "The Londoner," *The Bookman*, LXVI (March 1925), p. 49.

11. Edward Garnett, *The Golden Echo* (New York: Harcourt, Brace, & Co., 1954) p. 64.

12. Ford Madox Ford, *Return to Yesterday* (New York: H. Liveright & Co., 1932), p. 222.

13. Wells, *Experiment in Autobiography*, p. 531.

14. Joseph Conrad to W. H. Henley, in Frederick R. Karl, *Joseph Conrad: The Three Lives* (New York: Farrar, Straus & Giroux, 1979), p. 435.

15. Ford Madox Ford, *Ancient Lights and Certain New Reflections* (London: Chapman and Hall, Ltd., 1911), p. 198.

16. Ford, *Return to Yesterday*, p. 54.

17. Ibid., p. 188.

18. Joseph Conrad to Aniela Zagorska, in Frederick R. Karl, *Joseph Conrad: The Three Lives*, pp. 438–439.

19. Wells, *Experiment in Autobiography*, p. 525.

20. Joseph Conrad to H. G. Wells, May 25, 1898 (the archives of H. G. Wells, Champaign/Urbana, Ill.).

21. Ibid., October 11, 1898.

22. Ibid., November 17, 1898.

23. Ibid., undated.

24. Ford, *Return to Yesterday*, pp. 287–288.

25. Ford, *Joseph Conrad: A Personal Remembrance*, pp. 261–262.

26. Joseph Conrad to Ford Madox Ford, in *Return to Yesterday*, p. 54.

27. Ibid., pp. 190–191.

28. Joseph Conrad to William Blackwood, in Frederick R. Karl, *Joseph Conrad: The Three Lives*, p. 477.

29. Ford, *Return to Yesterday*, p. 190.

30. Ford Madox Ford, *The Cinque Ports* (Edinburgh and London: William Blackwood & Sons, 1900), pp. 162–163.

31. Ford, *Joseph Conrad: A Personal Remembrance*, p. 127.

32. Ford, *The Cinque Ports*, pp. 135–136.

33. Joseph Conrad, *Heart of Darkness* (New York: Doubleday, Page & Co., 1921), p. 219.

34. Ford, *The Cinque Ports*, pp. 90–91.

35. Ford Madox Ford to George T. Keating, July 27, 1923, in J. H. Morey, *Joseph Conrad and Ford Madox Ford: A Study in Collaboration*, p. 121.

36. Ford, *Return to Yesterday*, p. 189.

37. Joseph Conrad to J. B. Pinker, August 22, 1903, in Jocelyn Baines, *Joseph Conrad* (New York: McGraw-Hill, 1960), p. 292.

38. Ford, *Joseph Conrad: A Personal Remembrance*, p. 42.

39. Joseph Conrad to Ford Madox Ford, November 10, 1923 (New Haven: Yale University Library collection).

40. *Transatlantic Review*, Vol. I (January-February, 1924), pp. 98–99.

41. Joseph Conrad, in Zdzislaw Najder, *Joseph Conrad: Congo Diary and Other Uncollected Pieces* (Garden City, N.Y.: Doubleday & Co., Inc., 1978), p. 73.

42. Joseph Conrad and Ford Madox Ford, *The Nature of a Crime* (London: Duckworth, 1924), pp. xx–xxi.

43. Ford, *Joseph Conrad: A Personal Remembrance*, pp. 141–143.

44. Ibid.

45. Ford Madox Ford and Joseph Conrad, *The Inheritors* (London: Dent, 1928), p. 25.

46. Ibid., p. 74.

47. Ibid., p. 55.

48. Ford, *Joseph Conrad: A Personal Remembrance*, pp. 124–125.

49. Joseph Conrad, in Najder, *Joseph Conrad: Congo Diary and Other Uncollected Pieces*, pp. 117–118.

50. Conrad, in Frederick R. Karl, *Joseph Conrad: The Three Lives*, pp. 549–550.

51. Ford, *Return to Yesterday*, p. 196.

52. Ford, *Joseph Conrad: A Personal Remembrance*, p. 179.

53. Joseph Conrad and Ford Madox Ford, *Romance* (London: Dent, 1923), p. 32.

54. Ibid., p. 144.

55. Ibid., p. 169.

56. Ford, *Joseph Conrad: A Personal Remembrance*, pp. 16–17.

57. Ford, *Return to Yesterday*, pp. 187–188.

58. Joseph Conrad, *Typhoon* (New York: Doubleday, Page & Co., 1924), p. 19.

59. Conrad, *The Rover* (New York: Doubleday, Page & Co., 1924), p. 4.

60. Conrad, "The Return" in *Tales of Unrest* (New York: Doubleday, Page & Co., 1924), p. 123.

61. Conrad, *Heart of Darkness*, p. 220.

62. Ford, *Joseph Conrad: A Personal Remembrance*, pp. 192–195.

63. Wells, *Experiment in Autobiography*, p. 525.

64. Ford, *Return to Yesterday*, pp. 199–200. Translates: "Not bad, as a way to describe us."

IV. James and Wells

1. Henry James to William James, January 9, 1895, *The Letters of Henry James*, Vol. I, ed. Percy Lubbock (New York: Charles Scribner's Sons, 1920), p. 227.

2. H. G. Wells, "A Pretty Question," *Pall Mall Gazette*, January 7, 1895.

3. H. G. Wells, "Boon," in *Henry James and H. G. Wells*, eds. Leon Edel and Gordon H. Ray (Urbana: University of Illinois Press, 1955), pp. 248–249. This book is indispensable to any student of the question. As its subtitle suggests, it provides "A Record of their Friendship, their Debate on the Art of Fiction and their Quarrel."

4. H. G. Wells to Hugh Walpole, 1916, ibid., p. 39.

5. Rebecca West, *Henry James* (London: Misbet, 1916), pp. 107–108.

6. H. G. Wells to Henry James, July 8, 1915, *Henry James and H. G. Wells*, eds. Edel and Ray, p. 264.

7. Henry James to H. G. Wells, ibid., p. 267.

8. H. G. Wells to Henry James, *The Letters of Henry James*, Vol. II, ed. Lubbock, p. 488.

9. Henry James to H. G. Wells, *Henry James and H. G. Wells*, eds. Edel and Ray, p. 268.

10. H. G. Wells, *Experiment in Autobiography* (New York: The Macmillan Co., 1934), p. 508.

11. Henry James to William Dean Howells, January 22, 1895, *The Letters of Henry James*, Vol. I, ed. Lubbock, p. 230.

12. Henry James to H. G. Wells, December 9, 1898, *Henry James and H. G. Wells*, eds. Edel and Ray, p. 55.

13. H. G. Wells to Henry James, January 16, 1899, ibid., pp. 58–59.

14. Henry James to H. G. Wells, January 29, 1900, ibid., p. 63.

15. Ibid., June 17, 1900, p. 67.

16. Ibid., September 23, 1902, pp. 80–81.

17. Ibid., October 7, 1902, pp. 81–82.

18. Ibid., November 15, 1902, pp. 84–85.

19. Ibid., October 14, 1903, pp. 87–88.

20. Ibid., November 8, 1906, pp. 113–114.

21. Ibid., March 20, 1912, pp. 157–158.

22. H. G. Wells to Henry James, March 25, 1912, ibid., pp. 159–160.

23. Henry James to H. G. Wells, March 25, 1912, ibid., pp. 161–162.

24. Henry James to Edmund Gosse, March 26, 1912, ibid., pp. 163–164.

25. H. G. Wells, "The Contemporary Novel," a talk given to the Times Book Club in 1911, first printed in H. G. Wells, *An Englishman Looks At the World* (London, 1914), pp. 148–149, reprinted in *Henry James and H. G. Wells*, eds. Edel and Ray, pp. 154–155.

26. Joseph Conrad, in Norman and Jeanne MacKenzie, *H. G. Wells* (New York: Simon and Schuster, 1973), p. 241.

27. Henry James, "The Younger Generation," *The Times Literary Supplement*, March 19 and April 2, 1914, pp. 133–134 and 137–158, reprinted in *Henry James and H. G. Wells*, eds. Edel and Ray, pp. 182–183.

28. Ibid., pp. 189–190.

29. Ibid., pp. 191–192.

30. Wells, *Experiment in Autobiography*, pp. 412–413.

31. Ibid., p. 417.

32. Henry James to H. G. Wells, September 21, 1913, *Henry James and H. G. Wells*, eds. Edel and Ray, pp. 173–174.

33. H. G. Wells to Henry James, September 22, 1913, ibid., pp. 176–177.

34. Ibid., July 8, 1915, p. 264.

35. Henry James to H. G. Wells, July 10, 1915, ibid., p. 265.

36. H. G. Wells to Henry James, October 19, 1912, p. 169.

37. H. G. Wells, "Boon," in *Henry James and H. G. Wells*, eds. Edel and Ray, pp. 245–246.

38. Ibid., p. 242.

39. Ibid., pp. 240–241.

40. Ibid., pp. 247–248.

41. Ibid., p. 260.

42. Ibid., p. 253.

43. Henry James to H. G. Wells, July 6, 1915, *Henry James and H. G. Wells*, eds. Edel and Ray, pp. 261–262.

44. H. G. Wells to Henry James, July 8, 1915, ibid., pp. 262–263.

45. Henry James to H. G. Wells, July 10, 1915, ibid., p. 268.

46. Wells, *Experiment in Autobiography*, pp. 531–532.

47. James Joyce, *Letters of James Joyce*, ed. Stuart Gilbert (New York: The Viking Press, and London: Faber & Faber, 1957), pp. 274–275.

48. Henry James to H. G. Wells, July 10, 1915, *Henry James and H. G. Wells*, eds. Edel and Ray, p. 267.

V. Group Portrait

1. Rudyard Kipling, "Puck of Pook's Hill," *The Writings in Prose and Verse of Rudyard Kipling*, Vol. XXIII (New York: Charles Scribner's Sons, 1937), p. 275.

2. Ford Madox Ford, *Return to Yesterday* (New York: H. Liveright & Co., 1932), p. 27.

3. Marghanita Laski, "Domestic Life," *Edwardian England*, ed. Simon Nowell-Smith (New York: Oxford University Press, 1964), pp. 164–165.

4. Ibid., p. 182.

5. Frederick R. Karl, *Joseph Conrad, The Three Lives* (New York: Farrar, Straus & Giroux, 1979), p. 899.

6. Henry James to Joseph Conrad, November 1, 1906, *The Selected Letters of Henry James*, ed. Leon Edel (New York: Farrar, Straus, & Cudahy, 1955), p. 157.

7. Joseph Conrad, "The Nature of a Crime," in *Joseph Conrad, Congo Diary and Other Uncollected Pieces*, ed. Zdzislaw Najder (Garden City, N.Y.: Doubleday & Co., Inc., 1978), p. 118.

8. Derek Hudson, "Reading," *Edwardian England*, ed. Simon Nowell-Smith (New York: Oxford University Press, 1964), p. 315.

9. Joseph Conrad, "Henry James," *Notes on Life and Letters* (New York: Doubleday, Page & Co., 1924), p. 13.

10. William Faulkner, "William Faulkner's Speech of Acceptance Upon the Award of the Nobel Prize for Literature," *The Faulkner Reader* (New York: The Modern Library, 1959), p. 4.

Index